RAMBLING ORTZELS

by
PHYLO RAY

RAMBLING ORTZELS

by
PHYLO RAY

Railroad Street Press
394 Railroad Street, Suite 2
St. Johnsbury, VT 05819

Published in the United States by Railroad Street Press, St. Johnsbury, Vermont.

ISBN 9781936711154

1. Poetry

Jacket design by Susanna V. Walden.

Cover Art by Phylo Ray

First Edition 2011

Printed in the United States of America

Railroad Street Press
394 Railroad Street, Suite 2
St. Johnsbury, VT 05819
(802) 748-3551
www.railroadstreetpress.com

INTRODUCTION

A COURSE IN ORTZELS

THIS PUBLICATION OF "RAMBLING ORTZELS" IS THE FIRST NEST OF ORTZELS TO HAVE FLEDGED AND TO BE OPEN TO PUBLIC SCRUTINY. THE PRESENT FORMAT OF ORTZELS REMAINS CONSISTENT WITH ITS ORIGINAL STRUCTURE DEVELOPED OVER TWENTY YEARS AGO; A SIMPLE THREE LINE, FOURTEEN SYLLABLE POEM; THE FIRST LINE IS SEVEN SYLLABLES, THE SECOND LINE IS FOUR AND THE THIRD LINE IS THREE SYLLABLES IN LENGTH. THE VERY FIRST ORTZELS WERE SPONTANEOUSLY COMPOSED IN A FASHION WITHOUT FORETHOUGHT TO THEIR FORMATION NOR ANALYSIS OF THEIR CAUSE AND PURPOSE. VERY LITTLE HAS ALTERED THE METHOD IN WHICH ORTZELS ARE COMPOSED TODAY. CAREFUL OBSERVATION AND PRACTICE HAS HELPED TO BETTER UNDERSTAND THE COMPOSITIONAL THOUGHT FORM PROCESS THAT GOES INTO CREATING THESE APHORISTIC WORDS OF COMMENTARY.

RECENT DISCOVERIES HAVE BEEN ABLE TO ADD A CONSIDERABLE RANGE OF INSIGHT INTO THE IDENTITY AND LIFE CYCLE OF THIS LITTLE KNOWN LITERARY SPECIES. THE TECHNIQUE OF ORTZEL COMPOSITION IS KNOWN AS "ORTZELING." COMPOSITION OF ORTZELS IS ACCOMPLISHED BY TURNING THE INSPIRED; FOURTEEN SYLLABLE PHRASE AROUND IN ORDER TO INVESTIGATE POSSIBLITIES OF DEPTH INHERENT IN ITS ORIGINAL IDEA. THE ORIGINAL PHRASE IS ARRANGED INTO THE AFOREMENTIONED SYLLABIC STRUCTURE IN ORDER TO ACCOMPLISH IN SOME CASES AN "EPIGRAM" QUALITY; AS A SHORT, SATIRICAL SAYING INVOLVING A PARADOX.

THIS APPROACH TO "ORTZELING" OF TURNING THE PHRASE AROUND TO FIT THE ORTZEL FORMAT FACILITATES LANGUAGE LEARNING AND CREATIVE WRITING SKILLS. IDEAS PROCEED TO DEVELOPMENT TO COMPLETION EVOLVING WITH A COUNTERPOINT CONCEPT THAT ALTERS AND EXPANDS THE ORIGINAL IDEA. THE POTENTIAL OF ORTZELS TO DEVELOP INTO A RANGE OF CONCEPTS CONTAINING ALTERNATIVE MEANINGS CAN BE VIRTUALLY ENDLESS. SUCCESS IN ORTZELING DEPENDS UPON THE AUTHOR'S RESPONSE TO THE ORIGINAL IDEA INHERENT IN EACH VERSE; EMPLOYING THIS HINGE TO CREATE AN INFORMATIVE RESPONSE IN ORDER TO DETERMINE HOW WELL THE ORTZEL CAN FLY AND HOW FAR REACHING ITS IDEA TURNS OUT TO BE.

THE TYPICAL ORTZEL RENDITION OF A SATIRICAL STATEMENT APPEARS TO BE OBSCURE YET FAR REACHING; ITS ORIGIN IS TO BE FOUND WITHIN THE HUMAN IMAGINATION. THE FOLLOWING ORTZEL REFLECTS THIS IDEA IN AN ATTEMPT NOT ONLY TO PARAPHRASE IT BUT ALSO TO ELUCIDATE THE MEANING. HERE WE CAN SEE HOW ORTZELING FOCUSES ON A POINT OF PARTICULAR INTEREST IN ORDER TO IDENTIFY AND CLARIFY THE NATURE OF THE CRITTER THAT IS INSIDE US :

3/01/11

THE FAR REACHING DESTINY
OF ORTZELS IS
LODGED WITHIN

THE RECURRENT NATURE OF ORTZELING ALLOWS IDEAS AND WORDS TO REVOLVE BETWEEN ORTZELS' THREE LINES OF SEVEN, FOUR AND THREE SYLLABLES.

THE PROCESS OF TRANSFORMING WORDS AND IDEAS IN ORTZELING TAKES US BEYOND PRECONCEPTIONS WITH WORD SCULPTING TECHNIQUES TO CREATE AN INSPIRING EVENT INVOLVING A GREATER DISCOVERY OF OUR SELF. OUR IDEAS ARE RECREATED THROUGH DEVELOPING THE INNER WORKINGS OF OUR MIND'S EYE; TO ENJOY THE ENTERTAINING QUALITY OF THE PROCESS AND THE SOUNDS OF THE RECITED, SO CALLED "ORGELING ORTZELS."

VARIOUS LITERARY DEVICES DEPLOYED IN ORTZELING INCLUDES THE USE OF A PARADOX TO CREATE A SATIRICAL PHRASE; AND THIS APPEARS IN SPONTANEOUS RESPONSE WITH THE INTENT TO INSPIRE A SENSE OF HUMOR. AS YOU EXPLORE ORTZEL COMMENTARY; NEWLY INSPIRED IDEAS EMERGE THROUGH THE ORIGINAL INTENT OF EACH ORTZEL. MANY ORTZELS APPEAR TO BE HUMOROUS WHILE OTHERS CONTAIN ANOTHER RESPONSE IN THE FORM OF A SEED OF WISDOM .

THE INITIAL PURPOSE OF ORTZELING IS TO CREATE ORIGINAL IDEAS THAT CAN PROMOTE A GREATER SENSE OF SELF AWARENESS; TURNING WORDS AND IDEAS AROUND WITH THE USE OF SYNONYMS, ANTONYMS AND METAPHORS.

THE ORTZELING PROCESS OF WORD SCULPTING CAN OPEN UP POSSIBILITIES TO ENTER INTO HIGHER STATES OF THOUGHT. AS OUR ABILITIY TO PERCEIVE EXPANDS WITH THE CREATION OF ABSTRACT CONCEPTS. IDEAS CONTRARY TO MERE STEREOTYPICAL POINTS OF VIEW CAN EASILY BEGIN TO APPEAR . THE SPONTANEITY OF ORTZELING HELPS TO TURN WORDS AROUND TO FIT THE ORTZEL PHRASE STRUCTURE; INVENTING A TECHNIQUE TO GUIDE US IN OUR SEARCH FOR THE SYNTHESIS OF AN IDEA. ORTZEL'S ABILITY TO TRANSFORM IDEAS INTO EPIGRAMS AND APPHORISMS HAS EARNED THEM THE TITLE, "RAMBLING ORTZELS;" IN ORDER TO DESCRIBE THE

UNUSUAL NATURE OF THIS PARTICULAR COLLECTION OF POETRY.

AS THE ORTZEL EGG BEGINS TO HATCH WITHIN THE METAPHOR; ITS TRUE PURPOSE IS REVEALED IT EMERGES INTO THE WORLD OF THOUGHT WITH ALL OF THE POSSIBILITIES TO BECOME A SEED OF WISDOM AS WELL AS A SOURCE OF HUMOR. IN OUR QUEST FOR HUMOR; WE ENJOY THE FREEDOM OF ORGELING ORTZELS AS THEY ARE COMPOSED TO BE RECITED ALOUD. AN ENTIRELY OTHER SENSE OF SELF IS REVEALED TO US THROUGH THIS STUDY OF ORTZELS; A PATH OF DISCOVERY TO GREATER CONSCIOUSNESS TO SEE BEYOND THE QUANDRY OF OUR PRESENT LIFE'S DILEMMAS. THIS PROCESS MAY HELP US TO ALTER OBSOLETE CONCEPTS THAT HAVE PREVENTED US FROM TRANSFORMING OUR LIFE INTO AN APPRECIATION OF OUR ABILITY TO UNDERSTAND COMPLEXITIES WITHIN :

2/25/11

WE BECOME TRULY AMUSED
LEARNING TO LAUGH
WITH OUR SELVES

TO LAUGH WITH OURSELVES MAY INVOLVE SOME AWAKENING NO DOUBT; A MOST IMPORTANT STEP IN THE ABILITY TO DEVELOP GREATER UNSDERSTANDING. THIS PROVES TO BE THE DISTINCTIVE QUALITY OF ORGELING ORTZELS; AS OUR CAPACITY TO CREATE HUMOR HELPS US TO SEE A WORLD THAT WE MIGHT OTHERWISE HAVE MISSED; ONE WITH A RANGE OF KNOWLEDGE THAT WE PREVIOUSLY WERE INCAPABLE OF IMAGINING. OUR DOUBTS MYSTERIOUSLY VANISH WHEN WE TAKE THE INITIATIVE TO TRANSFORM OUR IDEAS AND ORTZELING DEVELOPS INTO A MOST

ENJOYABLE AND REWARDING EXPERIENCE; PROCESSING IDEAS TO PERCEIVE GREATER UNDERSTANDING AMIDST LIFE'S MANY LEARNING OPPORTUNITIES. TO EXPERIENCE ORTZELS' SIMPLE EXERCISES; WE TURN THOUGHT PROCESSES AROUND TO BRING THEM INTO FULL VIEW FROM A SAFE AND ENTIRELY NEW PERSPECTIVE. THIS REINVENTION OF OUR SENSE OF SELF EXPRESSION CAN INCLINE OUR MIND'S EYE TO FLOW WITH FRESH IDEAS; OFFERING MORE OF AN OPPORTUNITY FOR MIND BENDING EXPERIENCES THAT UPLIFT THE SPIRIT AND BROADEN OUR EVERYDAY EXPERIENCE WITH FRESH HONESTY AND OPENNESS.

CREATIVE WRITING HAS ALWAYS MAINTAINED POPULAR ACCLAIM IN THE ARTS AND HUMANITIES IN ITS QUEST TO REFORM EARTHLY EXISTENCE. SATIRICAL COMEDY DESIGNED SINCE ANTIQUITY HELPS TO STRENGTHEN THE COHESIVE QUALITY OF SOCIAL CULTURE; VIEWING PROBLEMS AND FACING THEM WITH A SENSE OF AWE. THIS METHOD OF SOLUTION CAN CREATE A REVELATION IN SOCIETY'S COLLECTIVE CONSCIENCE; RELIEVING STRESS AND CARVING CREATIVE IDEAS OUT OF DEAD WOOD.

AS INDIVIDUALS; WE TEND TO MASTER A CERTAIN IDENTITY THAT IS DEVELOPED THROUGHOUT OUR CHILDHOOD; BUT PERHAPS WE'VE BEEN HELD BACK IN OUR ABILITY TO APPRECIATE OUR GREATER INNATE SENSE OF HUMOR . AS WE AGE; WE DON'T ALWAYS HAVE THE NECESSARY OPPORTUNITES TO PROGRESS UPON THE PATH OF A HEALTHY MIND SET. TOO MANY PEOPLE HAVE TO CONTEND WITH RECURRING DIFFICULTIES INVOLVING SELF ESTEEM AND SELF INDUCED STRESS. IT IS OFTEN TOO EASY TO FALL VICTIM TO NEGATIVE THINKING INSTEAD OF SEARCHING FOR CREATIVE NEW SOLUTIONS IN PLAYING OUT DIFFICULTIES. THE TRICK IS TO ACCOMPLISH THIS PLAY WITHOUT BECOMING DAMAGED IN THE PROCESS.

ORTZELING IS DESIGNED TO ALTER OUR RELATIONSHIP WITH THE MUNDANE REALITY AND TO CONNECT US WITH THE LOST REMNANT OF OUR CHILDLIKE WONDER THAT LIFE HAS HIDDEN FROM US. PERHAPS WE'VE MISSED OUT TOO LONG AND NOW WISH TO BEGIN TO LOCATE SOME OF THE MISSING PARTS OF OUR LOST EXISTENCE. ORTZELS ARE OPEN TO THIS POSSIBILITY; PROVIDING A LINGUISTIC MEDIUM IN WHICH TO PRACTICE LITERARY AND MIND TRAINING SKILLS.

ORTZELING CAN RESEMBLE SKILLS INHERITED FROM ANCIENT TIMES OF ENORMOUS SPIRITUAL INNOVATION; SUCH AS THE FOURTH CENTURY A.D. VERSE KNOWN AS "HEPTOSYLLABIC COUPLETS" DEVELOPED BY A SPIRITUAL PILLAR OF THE EARLY CHRISTIAN FAITH; SAINT EPHREM OF SYRUS, FROM ANTIOCH IN ASIA MINOR. HE COMPOSED SACRED SCRIPTURE IN THE SYRIAC LANGUAGE; A DIALECT OF THE SAME "ARAMAIC" THAT JESUS OF NAZARETH GREW UP SPEAKING TO THE SOUTH IN ANCIENT JUDEA .

THE CHRISTIAN, MONASTIC SCHOOL IN WHICH SAINT EPHREM COMPOSED AND TAUGHT SCRIPURE; COMPOSED OVER THREE HUNDRED THOUSAND VERSE IN HEPTOSYLLABIC COUPLETS. THESE POEMS CONSIST OF DOUBLE LINES OF SEVEN SYLLABLE VERSE; TOTALLING FOURTEEN SYLLABLES PER COUPLET. COMPOSITIONS OF SAINT EPHREM ARE SOME OF THE EARLIEST KNOWN CHRISTIAN CHURCH HYMNODY; POETRY AND SERMONS ON ETHICS AND MORALITY COVERING A GREAT VARIETY OF SUBJECTS; VERSE THAT IS RECITED EVEN TO THIS DAY IN CHRISTIAN RELIGIONS AND CHURCHES.

ORTZELS ALSO CONTAIN FOURTEEN SYLLABLES; AND A SURPRISINGLY SIMILAR STRUCTURE TO THE HEPTOSYLLABIC COUPLETS OF SAINT EPHREM; THAT WERE DIVINELY INSPIRED VERSE WRITTEN OVER SIXTEEN HUNDRED YEARS PREVIOUS TO THE DISCOVERY OF

ORTZELS. ALTHOUGH ORTZELS HAVE HAD NO PREVIOUS KNOWLEDGE OF THE HEPTOSYLLABIC VERSE OF THE SCHOOL OF SAINT EPHREM; THE SYNCHRONICITY BETWEEN THEM AND ORTZELS' STYLE OF VERSE PROVIDES AN INTERESTING HISTORICAL FOOT NOTE.

OTHER ANCIENT CIVILIZATIONS AROUND THE GLOBE HAVE ALSO BENEFITTED FROM THE USE OF VERSE IN THEIR SPIRITUAL RITUALS. THE MOST ANCIENT RECORDED CIVILIZATIONS OF INDIA IN THE VALLEY OF THE INDUS RIVER REALIZED THE BENEFICIAL EFFECTS OF CHANTING PHRASES OF "SACRED SYLLABLE MANTRAS." THESE TRANSCENDANT CHANTS COMPOSED ORIGINALLY FOR VERBAL RECITATION DEVELOPED INTO THE "BAKTI YOGA" MEDITATIONS KNOWN AS "BHAJANA" AND KIRTANA." THIS CALL AND RESPONSE SINGING THAT IS POPULAR TO THIS DAY IN BOTH THE EAST AND WEST INSTILLS IN THE MINDS OF PARTICIPANTS A HEALTHY RESONANCE OF THOUGHT FORM FREQUENCY. THE PHILOSOPHY OF BAKTI YOGA IS BASED UPON THE CONCEPT OF PRAISING THE BENEFICIAL QUALITIES OF THE WORLD OF NATURE, AND THE UNIVERSE; THAT IS OUR NATURAL WORLD TO BE LOVED AND CARED FOR; AS OUR SINGLE SOURCE OF LIFE. THE BEINGS PRAISED IN THESE MANTRAS ARE SYMBOLIZED BY THE DIFFERENT ASPECTS OF THE GODS AND GODDESSES FORMING AN ART OF VERBAL AND VISUAL MEDITATION THAT CAN IMPROVE THE HEALTH OF THE INDIVIDUAL WHO WISHES TO ENHANCE THEIR MIND, BODY CONNECTION WITH YOGA; DIVINE UNION.

LANGUAGES THAT HAVE DEVELOPED OVER THE AGES SPECIFICALLY FOR THE BENEFIT OF HIGHER STATES OF CONSCIOUSNESS HAVE SURVIVED FOR THE PURPOSE OF BRINGING GROUPS OF PEOPLE TOGETHER IN CELEBRATION AND HEALING. ANOTHER POPULAR FORM OF POETRY; LIKE SACRED SOUND MANTRAS IS AN ANCIENT JAPANESE FORM OF VERSE KNOWN AS

"HAIKU." THIS ALSO CREATES A UNION BETWEEN NATURE AND THE HUMAN MIND. HAIKU POETRY HAS BECOME A POPULAR ART FORM IN JAPAN SINCE THE SIXTEEN HUNDREDS WHEN POETS LIKE "BASHO" BEGAN TO COMPOSE SHORT; SEVENTEEN SYLLABLE POEMS INSPIRED BY NATURE AND ITS CHANGING SEASONS. CURIOUSLY ENOUGH THE HAIKU CONSISTS OF A SEVEN SYLLABLE LINE SURROUNDED BY TWO, FIVE SYLLABLE LINES. SO HERE IS THE TOPICAL SEVEN SYLLABLE LINE APPEARING AS IF BY NECESSITY ONCE MORE; AS IN THE FOLLOWING EXAMPLE OF A HAIKU POEM :

SUNSET PINK BRANCHES
SNOW COVERED THE CHERRY TREE
ECHOES SPRING BLOSSOMS

WHEN APPLIED IN A POSITIVE MANNER; ORTZELING LIKE AN ANCIENT, SACRED LITERARY TECHNIQUE HAS POTENTIAL TO TRANSFORM THE HUMAN THOUGHT PROCESS INTO A PROFOUND POSITIVE EXPERIENCE AS IN THE FOLLOWING ORTZEL :

2/16/11

WORDS WILL ALWAYS WORK WITH SOUNDS
SINGING SACRED
SOUNDING THEMES

IT SEEMS AS IF EVERYTHING HAS BEEN DONE BEFORE IN A MYRIAD OF CONTEXTS FROM ANCIENT CIVILIZATIONS UP TO MODERN TIMES; AND THAT WE HAVE ONLY TO REINVENT THE PROVERBIAL WHEEL IN ORDER TO ENJOY THE EVOLUTION OF OUR HUMAN

LEARNING EXPERIENCE. INDEED EVERYTHING IS WAITING TO BE REDISCOVERED AND REINTERPRETED INTO A CONTEMPORARY GENRE OF CREATIVE EXPRESSION.

THE USE OF SATIRE IN THE HUMANITIES IS ONE SUCH WELL KNOWN TOOL EMPLOYED THROUGHOUT ALL GREAT LITERATURE TO CREATE A SHIFT OF CONSCIOUSNESS; BY INTRODUCING AN ALTERNATIVE THOUGHT FORM THAT INDUCES A STATE OF HUMOR. THE CASUAL TERM; "LIGHTEN UP" REFERS TO THIS STATE OF REDUCED STRESS THAT PERMIT'S CLEARER FORMS OF COMMUNICATION TO DEVELOP, LEADING TO GREATER FORMS OF COMPREHENSION.

A MORE RECENT EXAMPLE OF LITERARY SATIRE IN THE FORM OF A PROSE TECHNIQUE IS THE "PARAPROSDOKIAN." "PARA" IS THE GREEK WORD FOR "BEYOND" AND "DOKIAN" IS THE GREEK WORD FOR "EXPECTATION;" THIS MUST MEAN; "PROSE THAT GOES BEYOND EXPECTATIONS," (TO SURPRISE US BEYOND OUR PRECONCEPTIONS). THE PARAPROSDOKAIN FORM OF SATIRE INVOLVES THE USE OF CONTRADICTION TO CREATE A SUBTLE TWIST OF MEANING BETWEEN THE BEGINNING AND END OF THE PIECE; IN ORDER TO FORM A HUMOROUS ENDING THAT COMPLETES THE SATIRE. SOME ORTZELS SIMILARLY TURN A PHRASE TO CREATE COMMENTARY WITH A SATIRICAL TWIST; SO THEY MAY VERY WELL BE CONSIDERED TO BE "PARAPOEMDOKIANS;" A FREE VERSE OF STYLISTIC POETRY THAT MAKES USE OF CONTRADICTION TO CREATE SATIRE. THE ORTZELING PROCESS OF TURNING A PHRASE IN ORDER TO REVEAL THE PARADOXICAL SIDE OF THINGS GUIDES US INTO AN INTRIGUING PROCESS OF SELF DISCOVERY. THIS ENTAILS REACHING BEYOND OUR ORDINARY MINDSET IN ORDER TO FIND RELATED ASPECTS OF IDEAS FROM ENTIRELY UNFAMILIAR POINTS OF VIEW.

IN THIS RESPECT; ORTZELING BECOMES AN IMPORTANT TOOL FOR RETHINKING PROBLEMS AND DISSOLVING BLOCKS CALLED MIND LOOPS. BY LEARNING HOW TO TURN IDEAS AROUND WITH THE ORTZELING PROCESS; WE REFORM RECURRING NEGATIVE THOUGHT FORM PATTERNS THAT WERE PREVIOUSLY WASTING OUR TIME

BY TRANSFORMING THESE INTO CREATIVE THOUGHT PROCESSES WE BEGIN THE PRACTICE OF LEARNING TO SEE SITUATIONS FROM THE VANTAGE POINT OF THREE HUNDRED AND SIXTY DEGREES; AS WE BECOME AWARE OF OUR ABILITY TO BECOME THE SOLE INVENTORS OF OUR OWN POSITIVE THOUGHT PROCESSES (WELL ALMOST.)

THIS PROCESS MAY HELP US TO RECOGNIZE OTHER PEOPLE WHO ALSO THINK CREATIVELY AND WHO ENJOY SUCH WORD GAMES AS ORTZELING; LEADING TO SELF EMPOWERMENT WITH THE ABILITY TO RELEASE CERTAIN ATTACHMENTS AND AVERSIONS IN OUR LIVES THAT MIGHT UNWITTINGLY HAVE LIMITED US WITHIN A CONDITION THAT WAS LACKING THE FLOW OF THE KNOWLEDGE THAT WE DESIRE.

BY ENTERING THE "ORTZEL MIND SET"; WE BEGIN TO GENERATE IDEAS INTO THOUGHT FORMS THAT FLOW WITHIN THE STREAM OF CONSCIOUSNESS TO THE MIDPOINT WHERE INSPIRATION PLAYS UPON EXPERIENCE; CREATIING RESPONSE IN WHICH ORTZELS DISPLAY EVERY SIDE OF A SITUATION. CREATING SATIRE IS TO ENTER THE CONTRADICTORY NATURE OF THE HUMAN MIND AND TO OBSERVE THE WAYS IN WHICH THOUGHT FORMS AND IDEAS EVOLVE, SHIFT AND MANIFEST INTO PERSONAL POWER .

WHILE SOME ORTZELS COME PREPARED FOR THE FINAL PAGE; OTHERS MIGHT OFTEN INVOLVE A PERIOD OF TIME TO SET THE ORTZEL IDEA ASIDE IN ORDER FOR IT TO "COMPOST" OR GEL BEFORE IT METAMORPHOSES

INTO ITS FINAL IDEA AS AN ORGELING ORTZEL. AND BY TAKING OUR TIME; WE ARE ALLOWING OUR SELF AWARENESS TO HAVE THE OPPORTUNITY TO EVOLVE INTO A RANGE OF RELATED IDEAS THAT CREATE FULLY ROUNDED ORTZEL CONCEPTS.

A GOOD TIME TO BEGIN ORTZELING IS WHEN OUR MIND IS CLEAR OF DAILY CLUTTER; EARLY ENOUGH IN THE MORNING TO RELATE TO OUR DREAM WORLD. TECHNIQUES TO FREE US UP SUCH AS THE DAILY PRACTICE OF MEDITATION CAN PROVIDE AN EXCELLENT SOURCE OF CREATIVE STIMULATION. MANY AN INNOVATIVE TECHNIQUE CAN RECREATE THE HEART'S CONNECTION TO INSPIRE THOUGHT PROCESSES; MAKING IT SEEM AS IF ORTZELS HAVE THEIR OWN WAY OF PERCEIVING REALITY. THIS DISCIPLINE CAN TAKE US DIRECTLY INTO THE MIND'S CREATIVE FLOW; LOOKING FORWARDS TO THE GIFTS EACH NEW DAY HAS IN STORE.

RAMBLING ORTZELS ARE BEST READ INDIVIDUALLY; FIRST SILENTLY AND THEN OUT LOUD; IN ORDER TO ACHIEVE A FEELING FOR THEIR SYNTAX AND SOUNDS. THERE ARE SEVEN ORTZELS TO A PAGE IN THIS COLLECTION OF "RAMBLING ORTZELS;" SO THEY CAN EASILY BE STUDIED UNTIL ONE IS FOUND TO CONNECT WITH. THESE ORTZELS ARE CHRONOLOGICALLY ARRANGED AND DATED IN THE ORDER OF THEIR COMPOSITION. THERE IS NO PREARRANGEMENT OF SPECIFIC SUBJECT MATTER SO RAMBLING ORTZELS DO INDEED RAMBLE . THE COMPOSITION IS DESIGNED TO FACILITATE A CERTAIN SENSE OF DETACHMENT; THAT ONE MIGHT FIND IN A CROSS WORD PUZZLE. THIS QUALITY OF INDIVIDUALLY INDEPENDENT SUBJECT MATTER RETAINS THE AIR OF SPONTANEITY IN WHICH IT WAS COMPOSED.

ONE OF ORTZELS' LITERARY TOUR DE FORCE IS CONTAINED WITHIN ITS ABILITY TO SURPRISE US WITH

SUBTLE TWISTS OF MEANING; WHETHER IT BE IN SATIRE OR A PUN. AND THE SOUNDS OF THE ORGELING ORTZEL CAN BE AN ENTERTAINMENT IN ITSELF. THE OPPORTUNITY TO EXPERIENCE THEIR VOCAL SOUNDS ; ALONG WITH IDEAS EXPANDS OUR PERCEPTION TO OFFER GREATER INSIGHT; INVOLVING US IN OUR POTENTIAL FOR DISCOVERY OF PREVIOUSLY HIDDEN AREAS OF POTENTIAL SELF IDENTITY. THERE IS AN IMMENSE VARIETY OF IDEAS WAITING TO BE EXPLORED WITHIN THE ORTZEL FORMAT. WHILE ENGAGING THE COMMENTARY OF SPECIFIC PHILOSOPHICAL SUBJECTS ; ORTZELS CAN BE ENJOYED AS INSCRUTABLE RAMBING ORTZEL ENTITIES; BECOMING A SOURCE OF HUMOR IN THEIR OWN LIGHT. BY ENJOYING THEM AS THE SPIRIT MOVES US; WE LEARN TO LAUGH AWAY PROBLEMS; BECOMING FULLY AWARE OF THE ISSUES THAT HAVE CREATED OUR MENTAL BLOCKS AND MIND LOOPS.

AS WE CHOOSE TO ACKNOWLEDGE OUR INATE SENSE OF HUMOR; INSPIRATION BEGINS TO BUBBLE TO THE SURFACE; AS IT DOES FOR EXAMPLE IN THE ANCIENT PRACTICE OF "LAUGHING YOGA." THIS UNION OF DISCIPLINE PREDATES THE NEW TESTAMENT ERA BY PERHAPS EIGHT THOUSAND YEARS; PROVING THAT POSITIVE LAUGHTER HAS ALWAYS BEEN A MOST IMPORTANT TOOL IN CREATING CIVILIZATION. LAUGHING YOGA STIMULATES ALL THE HUMAN SENSES; ESPECIALLY THE HEALTHY, PHYSICAL FUNCTONING OF OUR INTERNAL ORGANS.

IN THE POWER OF MIND AND BODY EXERCISE, HAPPY LAUGHTER BRINGS OUR MENTAL AND PHYSICAL, AS WELL AS CONSCIOUS AND SUBCONSCIOUS ENERGIES INTO PLAY WITH A CERTAIN HOMOGENEITY OF PURPOSE . THIS ALSO HELPS THE INDIVIDUAL PERSONALITY TO BECOME WELL ROUNDED; OFFERING A FULL RANGE OF EXPERIENCE THAT IS MEANINGFUL TO LIFE. ORTZELING CAN REMOVE OUR LIMITATIONS BY

ACTING AS THIS KIND OF YOGA; TEACHING US TO CHALLENGE CONCEPTS THAT WE ARE NOT NORMALLY AWARE OF; IN THE WAYS IN WHICH WE LISTEN TO WHAT PEOPLE HAVE TO SAY IN EVERYDAY LIFE. TO CONSIDER IDEAS FROM THE POINT OF VIEW THAT EACH AND EVERY PHRASE MIGHT APPARENTLY HOLD SOME HIDDEN, MEANINGFUL GEM FOR US TO INVESTIGATE; THERE NOW APPEARS TO BE AN ENTIRELY NEW WORLD TO ENGAGE IN OUT THERE AND IN HERE.

PERHAPS WE DO NOT HABITUALLY INTEND TO IMAGINE THE ANTITHESIS OF WHAT WE HEAR THAT IS BEING SAID; ALTHOUGH A EUROPEAN THEOLOGIAN HAS REMARKED THAT; "WE FIND OUT WHAT SOMEONE IS THINKING BY WHAT THEY ARE NOT TELLING US ABOUT SOMETHING." BELIEVING WHAT PEOPLE SAY; WE FIND OUT ONLY WHAT THEY WANT TO TELL US BUT BY LISTENING TO HOW THEY ARE SAYING IT; THERE IS MUCH MORE TO LEARN IN UNCOVERING THE TRUTH OF THE MATTER. ORTZELING PROCESSES FACILITATE OUR ABILITY TO SEE AND TO ACKNOWLEDGE HIDDEN MEANINGS AND MOTIVATIONS IN THE USE OF WORDS.

THE TYPICAL RESPONSE TO ORTZEL PERCEPTION IS A SHIFT THAT CREATES THE EFFECT OF STOPPING OUR INTERNAL DIALOGUE LONG ENOUGH FOR OUR MIND TO UNWIND AND ADJUST INTO A STATE OF EQUIPOISE. PARADOXICAL STATEMENTS HAVE THIS TENDENCY TO PROVOKE OUR IMAGINATION INTO TAKING A SECOND LOOK AT THE MATTER; STIMULATING GREATER PERCEPTION IN ORDER TO ATTAIN DEEPER KNOWLEDGE AND UNDERSTANDING OF OURSELVES AND THIS WORLD.

ORTZELS CAN BE USED TO DEVELOP LYRICAL COMPOSITION. SONG WRITERS ARE OFTEN INSPIRED TO COMPOSE WORKS THAT BEGIN WITH A "HOOK;" AN ORIGINAL CATCH PHRASE THAT LEADS INTO THE SONG'S VERSE. THE HOOK MAY ALSO BECOME THE

THEME AND CHORUS OF A SONG. ORTZELING FACILITATES SONGWRITING SKILLS IN THE DEVELOPMENT OF A THEME ; DUE TO THEIR ABILITY TO ACT AS A "HINGE" THAT SWINGS IDEAS FREELY INTO FORMAT. THE FOLLOWING IS AN EXAMPLE OF A SONG COMPOSED IN THE FORM OF ORTZELS WITH THE USE OF A "HOOK;" TO BEGIN AND END THE SONG WITH. THIS INSPIRES THE THEME AND REVEALS AN "ORTZELING METHOD" OF SONG WRITING. THESE LYRICS MIGHT BE SUITED TO A MELODY IN THE MUSICAL STYLE OF A "GOSPEL BLUES" ARRANGEMENT :

2/03-17/11

WE KNOW OUR SAVIOUR HE IS
FROM GALILEE
WAY BACK WHEN

COMES AROUND MY DOOR BRINGING
HEAVENLY LOVE
OUR BEST FRIEND

TAKES ME TO THE WELCOME SHORE'S
HOLY WATER
TO BE CLEANSED

CARRIES US TO THE RIVER
OF FAITH HEALING
EVERY STEP

BRINGING THE HOLY SPIRIT
HEAVENLY LIGHT
BATHES MY HEAD

BLESSING MY SOUL WITH JESUS
IN FIRMAMENT'S
FOUNDATION

WE KNOW OUR SAVIOUR HE IS
FROM GALILEE
WAY BACK WHEN

ORTZELS CAN BE EMPLOYED IN A BROAD VARIETY OF LITERARY PURPOSE AS OUR PREVIOUS EXAMPLE OF THIS SEVEN SYLLABLE, MUSICAL VERSE ILLUSTRATES. THE STRUCTURE OF EACH ORTZEL ENCAPSULATES THIS PROTOTYPICAL, SEVEN SYLLABLE FORM; SET WITHIN ITS CONTEXT OF FOURTEEN SYLLABLES. IT CAN BE SURPRISING TO NOTE HOW COMMON IS THE USE OF SENTENCES AND PHRASES IN OUR LANGUAGE THAT CONTAIN EXACTLY SEVEN SYLLABLES.

THE CHARACTERISTIC NATURE OF ORTZELS SEEKS TO INITIATE TRANSFORMATIVE IDEAS THAT CREATE AND ARE CONTAINED WITHIN THEIR FOURTEEN SYLLABLE FORMAT. BUT NO ONE SEEMS TO KNOW WHICH COMES FIRST; THE ORTZEL OR THE FORMAT; THERE IS NO REAL NEED TO KNOW. ONLY BY TURNING THIS IDEA AROUND TO VIEW IT IN SIMPLIFIED COMPLETION CAN WE ALLOW INTUITIVE NATURE PLAY WITHOUR HARMONIOUS INTENT. THIS MIGHT NOT SEEM TO BE IMPORTANT, BUT THE FINAL RESULT IS EQUAL TO OUR INSPIRATION; SO WE LET OUR MUSE FIGURE THIS ONE OUT. WHETHER OR NOT THERE IS A SUCCESSFUL ATTEMPT MADE TO

TRANSMUTE WATER INTO WINE OR IDEAS INTO ORTZELS; IS DONE SIMPLY BY TAPPING INTO OUR OWN SOURCE TO DISCOVER WHAT'S GOING ON BENEATH THE SURFACE. BY HAVING FEW PRECONCEPTIONS OF WHAT OUR UNCONCIOUS THOUGHT PROCESSES MIGHT CONSIST OF; WE HAVE CHOSEN TO HEAR IN THE WAY OF "SEEING" THAT IS UNDERSTANDING WITH OUR INTUITIVE MIND. WE MIGHT ASK A QUESTION THAT DEALS WITH OUR ADDRESSING THE MUSE WITHIN AN ESOTERIC SENSE; AS WITH THE FOLLOWING TWO ORTZELS :

2/24/11

WHAT ARE THEY TRYING TO SAY
TELLING US IT'S
IMPORTANT ?

FORMING THOUGHTS THAT INTUIT
PROFOUND DEPTHS NOT
DISCOVERED ?

PERHAPS WE CAN SEE IN THE ABOVE TWO ORTZELS HOW "ORTZELING" HAS GUIDED US TO "A COURSE IN ORTZELS;" SOME PLACE DOWN THE FLIGHT PATH IN THE SENSE OF PROVIDING AN OBSERVATION WINDOW INTO THE COLLECTIVE CONSCIOUSNESS. EVENTS THAT WE WERE CONFUSED ABOUT IN THE PAST CAN BE OBSERVED IN A NEW LIGHT. OUR CIRCUMSTANCES IN LIFE CAN NOW APPEAR IN A MORE FAVORABLE LIGHT ONCE WE LEARN TO SEE THROUGH OUR SITUATION. AND CONSCIOUSLY CHOOSE TO ALTER OUR LIVES IN A POSITIVE MANNER.; NOW THAT WE BECOME AWARE OF THE RANGE OF IMPACT THAT OUR THOUGHTS HAVE

UPON OUR OWN BELIEFS, WE CAN MORE FULLY UNDERSTAND THE PURPOSE OF ORTZEL COMPOSITION AND TAKE THE TIME TO LET IDEAS DEVELOP THEIR FULL POTENTIAL AS PURVEYORS OF INSPIRATION. THIS PROCESS INVOLVES THE COMPOSTING AND WORD SCULPTING OF ORTZELS. WHILE GIVING OUR IDEAS TIME TO DEVELOP. THE COMPOSTING OF ORTZELS INCREASES OUR ABILITY TO ARRIVE AT A GREATER COMPREHENSION OF THE SUBJECT MATTER; PERCEIVING A HOLISTIC PICTURE OF EACH ORTZEL'S MESSAGE. THIS SERVES TO CONCEPTUALIZE INNER KNOWLEDGE IN SUCH A WAY AS TO PROVIDE GREATER INSIGHT INTO EVERY DAY EXPERIENCES.

THE FOLLOWING ORTZEL EXERCISE INVOLVES THE ABSTRACTION OF AN IDEA BEGINNING WITH A "SEED ORTZEL" THAT WAS RECORDED AND THEN RETURNED TO AT A LATER DATE TO ACT AS THE THEME FOR A SEQUENCE OF ESOTERIC ORTZELS.

THIS EXERCISE GIVES AN EXAMPLE OF AN EXTENDED ORTZELING TECHNIQUE IN WHICH SUBSEQUENT ORTZELS COMBINE WITH THE PREVIOUSLY RECORDED, ORIGINAL ORTZEL IN SUCH A WAY AS TO EXPAND THE THEME; IN THIS CASE OF A LUCID DREAM THAT INCLUDES A VARIETY OF SANDWICHES THAT APPEARED TO BE SWIMMING LIKE FISH; JUST BENEATH THE SURFACE OF THE BLUE WATER IN AN OLYMPIC STYLE SWIMMING POOL :

2/02/11

WE KNOW THAT ALL KINDS OF THINGS
APPEAR DEEPER
THAN OTHERS

4/23/11

THEY MIGHT TRULY INFORM US
TO REVEAL MORE
PROFOUND TRUTH

DISARMING THE MIND ITSELF
FROM FOMENTING
CONJECTURE

PREPARE TO GRASP WHAT THEY ARE
TRANSPARENTLY
PURSUING

SWIMMING TO EXIST INSIDE
THE SPACE BEYOND
REFLECTION

HERE THEY GUIDE US IN OUR SEARCH
TO LOCATE SOME
HIGHER TRUTH

THEY CAN APPEAR NOT TO BE
TOO DEEP FOR THOSE
WHO SEE THEM

THE ABOVE SET OF ORTZELS WAS SET ASIDE FOR OVER TWO MONTHS REQUIRING AN UNUSUALLY EXTENSIVE COMPOSTING AND WORD SCULPTING. THIS PROCESS HAS HELPED TO ARRIVE AT SOME

UNDERSTANDING OF THE DREAM'S SYMBOLISM AND INTENDED MESSAGE. THIS HAS CREATED A SURPRISE DEVELOPMENT THAT IS TYPICAL IN THE PARADOXICAL NATURE OF THE ORGELING ORTZEL; TO ACHIEVE AN EXPANSION OF THE ORIGINAL ORTZEL'S IDEA. TAKING THE TIME TO ALLOW IT TO COMPOST HAS INSPIRED A MORE IN DEPTH VIEW OF THE DREAM SITUATION AS PROBLEM SOLVING CAN OCCUR SUBLIMINALLY. THE ADAGE; "COUNT TO TEN BEFORE YOU LEAP" TENDS TO WORK MARVELS IN THIS CASE WHEN AN INTERIM EXPERIENCE CAN TAKE US BEYOND THE HANGUPS OF OUR PAST. TO BE PROVIDED WITH A FRESH VIEWPOINT THAT SURMOUNTS THE WALLS OF THE SUBCONSCIOUS MIND CAN BE AN ENCOURAGEMENT THAT HELPS US TO BE ABLE TO MOVE ON AND LOOK FORWARD TO FRESH NEW, LIFE CHANGING EXPERIENCES.

HERE WE COME FULL CIRCLE WITHOUT EVER HAVING TO DEAL WITH PREVIOUS ERRONEOUS NOTIONS OF OUR SELF IDENTITY IN REGARDS TO THE QUESTION OF DREAM PERCEPTION. WE CAN SEE THE ENTIRE ISSUE WITHIN OUR PERSONAL DEPTH; AND IT RESOLVES ITSELF SO REMARKABLY WELL THAT CONFRONTATION WITH PERSONAL IDENTITY BECOMES MERE WORD PLAY. AS THE FIRST ORTZEL IN THE ABOVE SET OF SEVEN ORTZELS OFFERS AN EXISTENTIAL OBSERVATION ON SELF AWARENESS; THE SEQUENTIAL SIX ORTZELS EXPAND THE ORIGINAL THEME WITH AN IN DEPTH VARIATION OF THE FIRST ORTZEL. THIS ORTZELING TECHNIQUE CREATES A WIDE RANGE OF RESPONSE IN ITS PURSUIT OF ALIGNMENT WITH THE ORIGINAL IDEA FACILITATING THE KIND OF MIND GAMES THAT ORTZELS LIKE TO PLAY; RAMBLING ALONG TO PROVIDE A BIRD'S EYE VIEW OF THE ORTZEL MIND SET. THIS ALLOWS US TO WITNESS THE SUBTLE SHIFT IN OUR OWN AWARENESS. WE BEGIN TO SEE HERE JUST HOW IT CAN BE THAT IDEAS SHIFT AND DISSOLVE

BLOCKS THAT HAVE HARBORED LIMITING IDEAS PREVENTING US FROM GOING FAR ENOUGH IN OUR PURSUIT OF KNOWLEDGE . THE FACT IS WE CAN NEVER GO TOO FAR IN OUR PURSUIT OF WELL BEING; FOR WE WILL ALWAYS END UP BACK WHERE WE BEGAN WITH A FRESH START. A LIFE THAT LEADS US AROUND BY THE NOSE UNTIL WE ARE EXHAUSTED MIGHT SUDDENLY CEASE TO BE A PROBLEM ONCE WE SUCCEED IN ACKNOWLEDGING DEEPER FORMS OF CONSCIOUSNESS.

SOLUTIONS CAN APPEAR WHEN WE HAVE THE OPPORTUNITY TO RELATE OUR FINDINGS WITH GREATER CONCEPTS OF REALITY; TO INVESTIGATE OUR OWN MENTAL MACHINATIONS IN ORDER TO DISCOVER IMPORTANT IDEAS HIDDEN IN THE DEPTHS OF OUR HEART AND MIND. ORTZELING APPEARS TO HELP US IN THIS PROCESS; REPLACING DILEMMAS WITH A MORE POSITIVE ATTITUDE. HERE IS AN ORTZEL THAT ADDRESSES THIS CONCEPT.

4/25/11

POSITIVE FEELINGS PLAY AN
INSTRUMENTAL
PART IN SONG

POSITIVE FEELING PLAYS AN INSTRUMENTAL PART IN LIFE AS WELL AS IN SONG. OUR INNER SONG CAN BE ENHANCED BY POSITIVE THINKING IN THE WAY THAT INSTRUMENTAL MUSIC CAN ENHANCE THE HARMONY OF A SONG. THIS HIGHER PURPOSE OF ORTZELING IS ALWAYS AVAILABLE IN THE PURSUIT OF WELL BEING.

IT IS REMARKABLE HOW THE SUBTLE USE OF WORD PLAY CAN PROVIDE AN OPEN ENDED SOURCE OF AWE; THAT MAKES US CAPABLE OF FACING LIFE'S CHALLENGES. BY DEVELOPING THE ORTZELING PROCESS;

OUR POINT OF VIEW CAN MATURE TO PROVIDE A MOST VALUABLE INFLUENCE CONCERNING SUCCESS IN LIFE; AS THE WAY IN WHICH WE DISTINGUISH OUR SELVES TO SHAPE IDEAS AND RELATIONSHIPS BECOMES A KEY FACTOR IN DETERMINING OUR ENJOYMENT OF LIFE.

OUR PERCEPTIONS ARE AN EXTENSON OF OUR HUMOR; AS OUR ATTITUDE CAN WORK TO TRANSFORM EACH EXPERIENCE POSITIVELY; ESPECIALLY ONES THAT APPEAR TO BE PSYCHOLOGICALLY CHALLENGING. AND BY TURNING THE PROBLEM INTO A LITERARY EXPERIENCE WITH ORTZELING; WE ARE EMPOWERING OURSELVES TO DELVE INTO UNKNOWN AREAS OF OUR THOUGHT PROCESSES; TO TRANSFORM THEM INTO A HIGHER PURPOSE. THE ORTZELS BECOME MESSENGERS WHO CAN BRING US TO THE POINT OF REMEMBERING WHO WE TRULY ARE WITH IN THE UNLIMITED FACETS OF OUR CREATIVE EXPRESSION; PERCEIVING THE WORLD BY LEARNING TO TRANSCEND ITS MORE LIMITING ASPECTS.

ORTZELING PERSONAL PROBLEMS CAN HELP US TO LIGHTEN UP SITUATIONS; IN FACT ORTZELS ARE NOT FULLY ACTIVATED THOUGHT FORMS UNTIL WE BECOME AWARE OF THEIR MEANING. THE WISDOM OF UNDERSTANDING THE WORLD OF DUALITY CAN TEACH US DISCERNMENT AND THE DIFFERENCE BETWEEN OUR LOWER AND HIGHER SELVES. THIS RELATES MORE DIRECTLY TO ALL THAT WE WANT TO LEARN IN LIFE; THAT DECISION MAKING MAY BE TAKING PLACE ON THE SUBCONSCIOUS LEVEL OF OUR MINDS AND THIS IS PRECISELY WHAT ORTZELS ARE TEACHING US; THAT THEY ARE NOT SIMPLY SITTING ON A BRANCH OF THE TREE OF LIFE; THEY HAVE FOUND THEIR WAY INTO THE TRUNK OF THE TREE OF LIFE TO RESIDE IN A SECURE NEST.

AN EXAMPLE OF THIS IDEA IS REPRESENTED IN THE THREE ORTZELS BELOW; ILLUSTRATED BY

CHARACTERISTIC ORTZEL RESPONSE ABOUT THE WAY IN WHICH ORTZELS VIEW THE WORLD AS AN EVER CHANGING IDEA. THIS LEADS NATURALLY TO FULFILLING ANSWERS THAT DEVELOP OVER TIME TO FORM AN EVEN MORE EXCITING QUEST. OF COURSE ON THE SURFACE; LIFE CAN APPEAR TO BE LIMITING UNTIL WE SEE IT IN AN UNUSUAL LIGHT. ORTZELS ARE VIEWED IN THE LIGHT OF NAÏVE EXPRESSION THAT ARE GENERALLY TIED UP WITH PERSONAL CONDITIONS.

THESE THREE ORTZELS SIMPLY ATTEMPT TO ELUCIDATE THE ISSUE OF THEIR OWN EXISTENCE :

2/07/11

WELL WE LIKE TO BE NAÏVE
MORE MILEAGE IS
WHAT WE GET

IS IT IN BLISS THAT NO ONE
EVER CARES TO
QUESTION IT ?

WE CAN GO ON FOREVER
DOING WHAT WE
LOVE TO DO

IT USUALLY DOESN'T TAKE TOO MUCH EFFORT TO HUNT DOWN THE POTENTIAL IDEA TO FORM AN ORTZEL. ALTHOUGH THE RESULTING ORTZEL MIGHT NOT HAVE A DIRECT SIMILARITY TO THE WORDING OF THE ORIGINAL SUBJECT; IT IS NOT IN THE BEST INTEREST TO IMITATE BUT INSTEAD TO INNOVATE UPON IDEAS THAT INSPIRE CREATIVITY.

ORTZELS CAN WORK FOR US AND FOR THIS PURPOSE THEY ARE BEST SUITED AS THEY ARE A PERSONAL ENDEAVOR TO COME TO GRIPS WITH REALITY IN A WORLD FULL OF CONTRADICTIONS. THEIR PURPOSE IS TO TEACH US HOW TO WORK WITH THE TRANSFORMATION OF IDEAS AS A PROBLEM SOLVING DEVICE; AND THIS INVOLVES THE DEVELOPMENT OF OUR CREATIVE THINKING. WHEN WE TAKE THE TIME TO STOP IN ORDER TO UNDERSTAND HOW THOUGHTS AFFECT BEHAVIOR ; ORIGINAL IDEAS CAN AUTOMATICALLY COME TO THE SURFACE . THE FOLLOWING ORTZELS CONSIDER THIS AND THE QUESTION OF OUR HUMAN RIGHTS AS WE ADDRESS THE ISSUE OF HOW WE MIGHT AFFECT OUR OWN FREEDOM OF THOUGHT PROCESS:

2/07/11

THE TRICKSER MIND MIGHT WANT TO
PLAY GAMES WITH OUR
LIBERTIES

INALIENABLE HUMAN
RIGHTS ARE HERE NOT
TO TRICK US

IT DOES MAKE US STOP TO THINK
WHAT WE SHOULD HAVE
THOUGHT ABOUT

WHAT IS LIFE WORTH IN THE END
WHO KNOWS DON'T WE
KNOW OUR SELVES ?

IF WE CAN READ BETWEEN THE
LINES THERE'S NOT TOO
MUCH FILLER

WAIT FIVE MINUTES TO SEE WHAT
LAWS CHANGE WE MIGHT
BE SURPRISED

A CONNECTION WITH THE SOURCE IN OUR OWN UNCONSCIOUS MIND CAN HAPPEN TO HELP US TO ENTERTAIN A "SACRED SPACE" THAT TAKES US BEYOND THE ORDINARY REALITY OF PRECONCEPTION. THIS CONNECTION IS OFTEN REFERRED TO AS OUR "MUSE;" WHO GUIDES US IN PURELY UNEXPECTED WAYS TO FIND A STREAM OF CONSCIOUSNESS ENABLING US TO RECEIVE THE GIFT OF CREATIVE KNOWLEDGE IN PURSUITS REQUIRING MORE INSPIRED THOUGHT. THIS PRACTICE OF ORTZELING IS DESIGNED FROM THE PERSPECTIVE OF A REALITY THAT IS "NON ORDINARY" AND MAGICAL IN NATURE . IT ENABLES US TO FUNCTION IN A CREATIVE WAY WITH GREATER FOCUS ON OUR IMAGINATION AS WELL AS IN A STATE OF JOY. HERE IS AN UNCHARACTERISTIC ORTZEL RESPONSE OF SARCASM IN RESPONSE TO THE ABOVE MATERIAL :

2/08/11

OH YES SUCH VERY DEEP STUFF
LAH TAH TYAH PLEASE
CONTINUE

ORTZELS CAN PROVE TO BE A MANIFESTATION OF THEIR OWN BIZARRE STYLE LIKE THE ONE ABOVE . THESE ARE SELECTED FROM THE TACKLE BOX OF LITERARY TECHNIQUE AS WE SEEK TO CATCH THE SALMON OF INNER KNOWLEDGE (AN ANCIENT MEPAHOR FOR INNER TRUTH.) THIS IS A MUCH SOUGHT AFTER PRIZE DESIRED BY EVERY ANGLING ARTIST IN PURSUIT OF INNER KNOWLEDGE. IT CAN BE COMPARED TO THE COSMIC RAY IN THE SEA OF UNIVERSAL CONSCIOUSNESS;WITHIN WHICH ARE FULLY FORMED, ORIGINAL IDEAS THAT ARE WAITING FOR US TO CATCH FROM THE ETHERIC REALMS OF OUR SUBCONCIOUS MIND. WE SIMPLY CAST OUR LINE OUT INTO THE DEPTHS WITH THE INTENT TO CATCH AN IDEA THAT IS READY AND WAITING. WE MIGHT EVEN GO DIVING INTO THE DEPTHS FOR ORTZELS; TO BE IMMERSED IN A FAVORITE FORM OF MEDITATION OR DREAMING IN ORDER TO PERMIT OUR SELVES TO ENGAGE MORE FULLY WITH THE STREAM OF INNER KNOWLEDGE WHERE OUR PRIZE CATCH AWAITS US. OUR MANIFESTATION OF ORTZELS WITH INTENT CAN OBTAIN SURPRISING RESULTS AS WE DEVELOP THE DISCIPLINE OF CREATIVE WRITING SKILLS AND EMPLOY POSITIVE THINKING TECHNIQUES THAT WE ARE GUIDED TO IN OUR PRACTICE. THE LEARNING AND ACHIEVEMENT BECOMES ONE AND THE SAME THING AS IN THE FOLLOWING ORTZEL :

2/08/11

LEARNING TO FOCUS ON THE ATTAINABLE HOOKS BIG FISH

ENTIRE SCHOOLS OF FISH ARE READY FOR THE EXPERT ANGLER IN THE FORM OF BRILLIANTLY COLORED SCHOOLS OF THOUGHT FORMS WITH COLORFUL SHAPES AND DIMENSIONS TO CHOOSE FROM. ONCE THE FISH IS CAUGHT AND SELECTED; IT MUST BE PREPARED FOR THE TABLE IN SOME NOVEL FASHION; WHETHER BROILED, PAN FRIED, BAKED OR TO BE SERVED UP AS SUSHI; CERTAIN DISCIPLINES ARE TO BE MASTERED BY PRACTICING THE ORTZELING PROCESS UNTIL WE EXPRESS EXACTLY WHAT WE FEEL . WORD SMITHING ORTZELS PLAYS A TRANSFORMATIVE ROLE IN REVEALING THE BEAUTY OF OUR IDEAS BY WAY OF THE CONTINUOUS LEARNING EXPERIENCE. FINDING OUR SELVES IMMERSED IN THE PROCESS OF OBSERVING IDEAS BEING CREATED WITH OUR MUSE IN THE SUBCONCIOUS MIND IS AN AWAKENING OF SORTS. AN IDEA THAT HAS LAIN DEEPLY HIDDEN AND FORGOTTEN FOR MANY YEARS MAY PRESENT ITSELF AFRESH IN A NEW LIGHT TO ILLUMINE US :

3/12/96

A BEAUTIFUL FLAME OF LOVE LIGHTS THE PATH OF HEART'S DESIRE

ORTZELING PROVIDES TECHNIQUES TO REVEAL THE SECRETS INHERENT IN ALL FORMS OF COMMUNICATION. THE WAYS IN WHICH WORDS ARE USED TO CREATE COMPLEX, DOUBLE MEANINGS FOR

INSTANCE; AS IN AN EPIGRAM PROVES TO BE AN INHERENT NATURE OF ORTZELS. ALTHOUGH THE DEEPER MEANING AND PURPOSE OF ORTZELS TENDS TO BE SELF EVIDENT IN THE EYES OF THE AUTHOR; IT CAN BE INITIALLY OBSCURE TO SOMEONE NOT FAMILIAR WITH THE ORTZEL STYLE UNTIL IT IS EXPLAINED AND THEN IT BECOMES ENJOYABLE QUITE EASILY

COLLECTING THEME MATERIAL FOR ORTZELING CAN BECOME AN ACTIVITY IN ITSELF; EVERY POET, SONG WRITER OR NOVELIST CAN DEVELOP DIRECT CONTACT WITH EXPERIENCES TO DRAW FROM IN THEIR SPECIFIC CREATIVE ENDEAVOR . ONE'S AQUAINTANCES MIGHT INVOLUNTARILY BEGIN SPOUTING AN ORTZEL SOUNDING PHRASE WHEN CAUGHT IN A STATE OF FRIENDLY CONVERSATION. PERHAPS AN ORTZEL GEM WILL UNEXPECTEDLY DROP LIKE AN EGG INTO YOUR NEST. AS THEY WATCH YOU WRITE DOWN WHAT THEY HAVE JUST SAID; TELL THEM THAT YOU ARE SIMPLY JOURNALING. AN AQUAINTANCE MIGHT BECOME UNEASY WATCHING YOU WRITING DOWN A PHRASE THAT YOU MIGHT ASCRIBE TO THEM WHILE OTHERS MIGHT BE FLATTERED. PERHAPS THEY IMAGINE YOU TO BE SPYING ON THEM; WORKING FOR THE GOVERNMENT OR SOMONE LACKING MORALITY. YOU CAN TELL THEM THAT THERE IS NO GUILT INVOLVED IN THE ORTZELING PROCESS AND THAT YOU ARE NOT EVEN QUOTING THEM DIRECTLY. IN MOST CASES YOU CAN CONTINUE TO HAVE A CIVIL CONVERSATION WITH YOUR FRIENDS AND BE FULLY ENTERTAINED AS WELL . WE TEND TO STIMULATE EACH OTHER WITH OUR IDIOSYNCRASIES AND THIS HELPS US TO BROADEN OUR PERSPECTIVE ON CERTAIN ISSUES; THOUGH NOT USUALLY ON ISSUES RELATING TO CONSPIRACY BASED THEORY. BE CAREFUL TO KEEP YOUR HANDS TO YOURSELF WHEN DEALING WITH CONSPIRACY THEORISTS UNLESS SOMEONE WANTS TO GIVE YOU HUG AND THEN YOU MIGHT

WANT TO COMPLY.

OUR OWN MUSE PLAYS A MAJOR ROLE OF INSPIRATION; OFTEN TIMES GUIDING US INTO THE STRANGEST PLACES THAT TEST OUR RESOLVE TO INCREASE LEARNING POSSIBILITIES. SO BEWARE OF THE ORGELING ORTZEL AND ITS HIGHLY ATTUNED RESPONSIVENESS TO OUR INTENT.

BY FAR THE MOST RELIABLE METHOD OF COLLECTING ORTZELS IS OUR OWN SOURCED AND COMPOSTED MATERIAL; THE STUFF THAT SPRINGS FROM IDEAS THAT MAY HAVE LAIN BURIED INSIDE US FOR DECADES; AWAITING SOME FORM OF RESOLUTION TO BURST THE BONDS OF FORGETFULNESS; YET WITHOUT THE SLIGHTEST INKLING THAT THEY COULD POSSIBLY BECOME AN INSPIRATION TO US.

MEDITATION IS AN EXCELLENT SKILL IN ACHIEVING ACCESS TO THE HIDDEN TREASURES OF OUR INNER KNOWLEDGE. EVERYONE MEDITATES TO SOME DEGREE AS ONE PATH TENDS TO LEAD TO ANOTHER; AND SOMETHING IN US ALREADY KNOWS ALL THERE IS TO KNOW ABOUT THIS LIFE. IT IS ONLY THE JUNK THAT NEEDS TO BE REMOVED TO OPEN THE DOOR TO OUR HIGHER SELVES.

IT IS FREEING TO SET ORTZELS ASIDE FOR AWHILE; TO ALLOW FOR THE COMPOSTING TO TAKE PLACE BEFORE ACCOMPLISHING A FINAL WORD SMITHING; FORMING THE SEMI MOLTEN ORTZELS INTO RECOGNIZABLE INSPIRATIONS. WE TEND TO KNOW WHEN THOUGHT FORMS RING TRUE AS THE ORTZEL COMMENCES ITS ORGELING; THAT CAN BE DESCRIBED AS A POSITIVELY MAGNETIZING EXPERIENCE.

AN EXAMPLE OF THIS SPONTANEOUS UNDERTAKING OCCURRED THIS MORNING; IN THE DEPTHS OF A NEW ENGLAND WINTER IN THE NORTH EAST KINGDOM OF VERMONT. AN OLD BRIEFCASE THAT HAD GONE UNOPENED FOR SEVERAL YEARS YEILDED A

FORGOTTEN, BLACK SPIRAL NOTE BOOK. UPON OPENING;TO REVEAL NOTES OF A LUCID DREAM THAT REPRESENTS A TIME OF IMPORTANT PERSONAL INTERFACE WITH SPIRITUALITY; A SOUL SONG OF NATURE SPIRITS IN WHICH THE FOLLOWING VERSES OF EXPANDED ORTZELS PROVIDE AN ACCURATELY PARAPHRASED ACCOUNT OF A LUCID DREAM. THIS COMPOSTED FOR A NUMBER OF YEARS AWAITING THE ORTZELING PROCESS TO REVEAL ITS SPIRITUAL MESSAGE ONCE AGAIN :

3/17/11

MELT THIS COLD WIND BLOWING HERE
WITH SUN SHINING
FROM THE SOUL

WATCHING CLOUDS FLY WITH GENTLE
BREEZE FOLLOWING
THE RHYTHM

PICK UP YOUR FEET THUNDER DANCE
SEE LIGHTENING BOLTS
EXPLODING

IN YOUR HEART OF GOLDEN LIGHT
ENERGY FOR
EARTH BELOW

DANCING WITH THE WEATHER SPRITES
LIBERATING
SACRED GROUND

ORTZELING IS INSTRUMENTAL IN DEFINING THE THEME OF THE LUCID DREAM. IT NOT ONLY ACTS AS A PARAPHRASING DEVICE BUT ALSO TIES THE ACTION AND THEME TOGETHER WITH STYLISTIC DEVICE.

THE EXPANSION OF AN ORTZEL THEME CAN ALSO APPEAR FROM ANOTHER, IMMEDIATE PERSPECTIVE AS IN THE NEXT EXERCISE; WHERE SEVEN OF THE EIGHT ORTZELS ARE DERIVED FROM AN INITIAL ORTZEL :

3/30/11

WE MIGHT WANT TO WAKE UP IN
A CERTAIN SPACE
AT THIS TIME

WE'RE ALREADY AWAKE BUT
HAVE NOT OPENED
OUR EYES YET

COME AGAIN IN ORDER TO
RE EMERGE IN
THE RIGHT WAY

COURAGE PROVIDES A NOVEL
SIGHT RESTORED TO
BRIDGE THE GAP

DANCING THROUGH LIFETIMES BRINGS SOME
INSIGHT OUT OF
IGNORANCE

LIVING OUR CONCEPTIONS OF
CREATION THROUGH
TOLERANCE

PERCEIVING A KINDER WORLD
ALTERING SOUL
REVERIES

TO CONTINUE DREAMING IN
THE FUNCTION OF
PURE WISDOM

THIS SET OF ORTZELS INVOLVES THE IDEA OF UNKNOWN CONCEPTS THAT EXIST WITHIN THE UNIVERSAL UNCONCIOUS MIND. OUR PURPOSE OF ORTZELING HERE IS TO FIND THE HIDDEN MEANING IMPLIED IN THIS SET OF ORTZELS; WHERE THE INSPIRATION OF THE FIRST ORTZEL DEVELOPS A PARTICULAR RELATIONSHIP WITH THE CONSECUTIVE SERIES; STIMULATING FURTHER, THIS DREAM THEME :

4/07/11

THE DREAMING THAT'SIMPLIED HERE
RELATES TO THE
SACRED PATH

ORTZELS PRETTY WELL SUM UP THEIR OWN NATURE IN THEIR ABILITY TO FACE CONTROVERSY; THAT IS TO TURN THINGS AROUND UNTIL THE SOLUTION BECOMES EVIDENTLY ANOTHER MATTER FOR SCRUTINY AND PERHAPS A MATTER OF SUBTLE HUMOR. ORTZELS POSE THE KINDS OF QUESTIONS THAT CAN PLUMB A SOLUTION; TO INVESTIGATE SOME BASIC PRECEPTS OF TRADITIONAL PHILOSOPHICAL THEORY :

4/07/11

DID ADAM AND EVE FALL WHEN THE UNIVERSE WAS FASHIONED ?

THE QUESTION THAT THIS ORTZEL POSES IS WHETHER OR NOT MODERN CHRISTIAN THEOLOGICAL DOCTRINE MIGHT CONSIDER A POTENTIALLY CONTROVERSIAL TWIST TO THE ACCEPTED STORY IN "GENESIS" OF THE CREATION OF MAN AND THE NATURE OF ORIGINAL SIN. QUESTIONS OF THIS NATURE CAN

POTENTIALLY LEAD TO A DRAMATIC PARADIGM SHIFT IN MODERN RELIGIOUS THOUGHT; PERHAPS POSING A MAJOR SHIFT IN THE NATURE OF THE CHRISTIAN FASHION INDUSTRY; THE QUESTION IS WHETHER INDEED THE HUMAN SOUL HAD SEPARATED FROM GOD BEFORE GARDENS WERE EVEN CREATED AND FRUIT BECAME FASHIONABLE OR WHY THESE WERE MADE AND DREAMED UP IN THE FIRST PLACE ? MIGHT THE ORIGINAL SIN AND ITS ACCOMPANYING GUILT COMPLEX BE LABELED AS A MERE "ORT" OF A MUCH LARGER SCHEME THAT EGO MANIPULATES; IN ITS EFFORT FOR US TO REMAIN SUSPENDED IN THIS MATERIAL STATE OF SEPARATION FROM THE TRUTH OF THE HOLY SPIRIT?

IDEAS LIKE THIS CAN BE ADDRESSED QUITE EASILY WITH ORGELING ORTZEL COMMENTARY; WHERE POSTULATIONS THAT ARE BASED UPON CONTEMPORARY THEORIES ASK QUESTIONS CONCERNING, FOR INSTANCE THE DIFFERENCE BETWEEN GOD'S GARDEN OF EDEN AND APPLE TREES IN OUR OWN BACKYARD. PERHAPS THE PROCESS OF ORTZELING IDEAS SUCH AS THESE CAN ASSIST US IN DETERMINING OUR OWN TRUE NATURE.

ANOTHER ORTZEL REFERENCES THE NATURE OF OUR EXISTENCE BY POSING THE QUESTION OF MEDITATION FROM A BUDDHIST PERSPECTIVE; THE CONCEPT OF ACHIEVING UNIVERSALITY THROUGH A STATE OF NON BEING OR THE EGO LESS STATE OF AN ALTERED CONSCIENCE THROUGH THE DAILY PRACTICE OF MEDITATION; IN WHICH THE WALLS OF FEAR BASED THOUGHT ARE REMOVED ONE BRICK AT A TIME; TO TRANSCEND THE LIMITING EXISTENCE OF OUR EGO. THE FOLLOWING ORZTEL'S IDEA TAKES US BEYOND THE EGO INTO OUR ATTAINMENT OF EQUANIMITY :

4/06/11

PROBLEMS CEASE TO EXIST WHEN
WE MEDITATE
BEYOND IT

ORTZELING CAPTIVATES PERSONAL QUESTIONS THAT HAVEN'T BEEN PREVIOUSLY DREAMED UP; IDEAS THAT DEAL DIRECTLY WITH OUR TRUE EXISTENCE. THE TREATMENT OF THESE BASIC ISSUES INVITES A GREATER POWER OF QUESTIONING INTO UNKNOWN REALMS OF THOUGHT PROCESSES. THE GIFTS OF KNOWLEDGE CONTAINED WITHIN ORTZELS CAN BE FOUND ALMOST ANYWHERE; INSIDE A NEWLY DISCOVERED NEST :

4/14/11

A COZY FEATHERED NEST TO HATCH OUR EGGS OF KNOWLEDGE IN

THIS ORTZEL CONTAINS AN IDEA THAT CAN TAKE US BEYOND THE PONDEROUS QUALITY OF THOUGHT; THE FEAR BASED PANDORA'S BOX THAT HAS SO CONFUSED THE MIND OF WESTERN HUMANKIND SINCE ANTIQUITY; A PLACE IN THE ORTZELS' NEST IN WHICH TO HATCH IDEAS TO RAISE US BEYOND THE LIMITS OF OUR PRESENT DILEMMAS. WE CAN BEGIN TO SOLVE EACH THOUGHT COMING ALONG ITS DISCURSIVE WAY; THAT IS HEADED FOR A COLLISION COURSE WITH REALITY; AND TO SEE HOW IT IS TO BE DEFLECTED AND TRANSMUTED INTO A TIMELY ORTZEL TO ACCELERATE US UPON OUR OWN TRUE PATH TO SELF REALIZATION.

THE ORTZEL PATH IS A SIMPLE WAY TO GO FORWARD; LIKE THROUGH A MOUNTAIN PASS INTO THE RARIFIED AIR OF WILDERNESS. TO FIND ORTZELS HATCHING EGGS INTO NEW IDEAS IN ORDER TO BRING THEM INTO THE LIGHT OF DAY. THE KNOWLEDGE STIMULATED BY ORTZELING OPENS UP A PERSONAL LEARNING EXPERIENCE THAT TAKES PLACE IN THE SECRET AREAS OF THE MIND; CONNECTING US TO ALL SENTIENT BEINGS AND PROVIDING US WITH A HEARTFELT INVITATION TO EXPLORE AND ENJOY OUR OWN DEVELOPING AWARENESS. AS ORTZELS BEGIN

TO EMERGE AND WE APPEAR WITH THEM; THEY REVEAL EVERYTHING TO DO WITH POSITIVE THINKING AS WELL AS THE ACCOMPANING ENERGY THAT OUR POWER OF THOUGHT PROJECTS; TO ATTRACT OUR EVENTUAL SUCCESS. WHETHER OUR INTENTIONS MANIFEST IN A POSITIVE OR NOT SO POSITIVE LIGHT; WE

CAN SEE BEYOND OUR IMMEDIATE RESPONSE TO THE SOLUTION OF OUR PROBLEMS; TO RECOGNIZE THE LEARNING POSSIBILITIES IN LESSONS THAT LINK US TO POSITIVE CHARACTERISTICS OF THE NATURE OF LIFE ON THIS PLANET; SO THAT REVERSALS THAT INTRUDE INTO THE HERE AND NOW ARE OBSERVED IN PERSPECTIVE:

4/30/11

REVERSALS INTRUDE INTO
OUR LIVES BUT WE
DON'T TRUST THEM

HERE IS AN ORTZEL THAT REFLECTS THE "GOLDEN RULE" OF BUDDHISM; "DO UNTO OTHERS AS YOU WOULD HAVE THEM DO UNTO YOU." AND REFERS TO THE CONCEPT AND IDEA OF "BUDDHA" AS AWAKENED AWARENESS. WE NEED NOT DOUBT OUR OWN SELF AWARENESS AND THE CHARACTERISTIC NATURE OF OUR PLANETARY EMBRACE OF CONSTANT CHANGE. THIS ORTZEL EMPHASIZES THE NECESSITY TO MAINTAIN A POSITIVE ATTITUDE AT ALL TIMES SO THAT WE DO NOT MISS THE MAIN POINT OF OUR EXISTENCE; THAT IS TO EXPERIENCE LIFE IN A STATE OF AWE AND WONDER. THERE IS NO NEED TO MAKE ANY ATTEMPT TO ELIMINATE THE VERY THINGS THAT CAN BEST TEACH US ABOUT THE IMPORTANCE OF LIFE :

5/11/11

HOWEVER DON'T SAY BUDDHA
DID IT WRONG NO
MORE BUDDHA

THE IDEA OF OUR BELIEF SYSTEM PLAYING A MAJOR ROLE IN OUR LIVES CAN BE SEEN IN CHRISTAIN THOUGHT AS WELL AS IN BUDDHIST THOUGHT. THE CHRISTAIN CREATION MYTH CONCERNING THE WELL KNOWN FRUIT OF THE TREE OF THE KNOWLEDGE OF GOOD AND EVIL IS CONSIDERED AS AN APPLE IN THE FOLLOWING:

5/11/11

WAS GOD IN THE APPLE OR
WAS THE APPLE
INSIDE GOD ?

EVE LOST THE APPLE SHE WAS
CONTENT FEASTING
ON ITS SOUL

WHAT VARIETIES CAN BE
GROWN TO SUSTAIN
THE GARDEN ?

GOD COMES INTO THIS GARDEN
CAN WE SOJOURN
HERE AS WELL ?

DON'T FORGET TO SPEND YOUR TIME
FILLED WITH TRUST BE
PASSERS BY

ORTZELS CAN BE ALL ABOUT FINDING FAITH IN ONE'S HIGHER SELF ALTHOUGH MANY MISTAKES ARE CERTAINLY MADE. WE PREFER TO ENGAGE WITH OUR MUSE TO HAVE AN AMUSING AND CONSTRUCTIVE DAY WORKING WITH GOOD IDEAS.

ORTZELS APPEAR NOT TO BE LIMITED TO THEIR SEVEN; FOUR; THREE SYLLABIC STRUCTURE. ALTHOUGH "RAMBLING ORTZELS" CONTAIN THISCONSISTENT FORMAT THROUGHOUT THE TEXT; THEY MIGHT AS EASILY INCORPORATE A SEVEN; THREE; FOUR SYLLABIC STRUCTURE; IN ANOTHER CADENCE OF VERSE. ORTZEL FORMAT PROVIDES THIS VERSATILITY IN SYLLABIC STRUCTURING TO FACILITATE POETIC EXPRESSION; AND THIS IS DEMONSTRATED IN THESE ORTZELS :

6/30/11

HARNESSING CRYSTAL POWER
DEFINING
INTUITION

DOES RESPONSIBILITY
ASSUME THAT
WE ARE IN CHARGE ?

SHE BUYS BREAD AND STROLLS ACROSS
THE BRIDGE TO
GRANDMOTHER'S HOUSE

NO NEED TO BUY BREAD GRANDMA
BAKES HER OWN
DELICIOUS LOAF

THERE SEEMS TO BE SOMETHING MORE PROSAIC ABOUT THESE ORTZELS ENDING IN FOUR SYLLABLES THAN THE ORTZELS ENDING IN THREE . THE FOUR SYLLABLE ORTZELS TEND TO HAVE A LESS SUCCINT SOUND THAN ORTZELS ENDING IN THE SHORTER, THREE SYLLABLES CONTAIN. THERE MAY BE AN ADVANTAGE IN THE DEVELOPMENT OF VARIOUS DIFFERENT STYLES OF COMPOSITION; CONSIDERING THEIR POTENTIALLY DIFFERENT RHYTHMS IN RELATION TO COMPOSING LYRICAL WORKS FOR INSTANCE.

INSPIRATION CONTAINED IN THE MAIN TEXT HAS DEVELOPED DRAMATICALLY OVER TIME; GERMINATING THE SEEDS IN THEIR MOST NATURAL, CREATIVE FLOW. THIS TEXT HAS TURNED OUT TO BECOME A JOURNAL OF SORTS; AN EXPRESSION THAT CONTINUES TO PROVIDE TRANSFORMATIVE ENTRAINMENT THROUGH CONTACT WITH THE MUSE. ORTZELING IS ONE SIMPLE VEHICLE USED TO GLEAN SOME KNOWLEDGE FROM THE SOURCE WITH OUR THOUGHT GATHERING. THROUGH THE MASTERING OF THESE THOUGHT PROCESSES; THE INTENT TO CREATE A BROADER UNDERSTANDING OF OUR HIGHEST PURPOSE IS EXPLORED IN LIGHT OF KNOWLEDGE :

6/30/11

WE HAVE FOUND THIS EPITOME'S
ILLUSIONS TO
PURELY SERVE

OUR FATHER'S FORM IS HERE TO
AMUSE MOTHER'S
INTENTION

ARE WE SURPRISED TO FIND THAT
THE UNIVERSE
HAS A VOICE ?

THERE IS MANY AN UNLIKELY SOURCE FOR ORTZELS THAT WILL POP UP AS IF A MAGICAL TOASTER HAS BEEN SECRETLY INSTALLED SOMEWHERE NEARBY; IN ORDER TO PROVIDE INSPIRATION FOR OUR STUDY OF EVERYDAY LIFE. SOME INEXPLICABLE THREAD EXISTS WITHIN OUR ARRAY OF SELF EXPRESSION WITH ITS THEME; AS THE STAGE OF OUR LEARNING PROCESS ENTERS THROUGH THE DOOR OF IMAGINATION. WE HAVE UNDERSTOOD THE PROCESS OF ACCUMULATING, VIEWING AND THE RELEASE OF IDEAS UNTIL THEY ARE TRANSFORMED INTO TRANSCENDENT CONCEPTS TO THE POINT OF DISTINGUISHING THE ORTZEL AS A PURE VEHICLE OF EXPRESSION :

10/24/11

WE SEE THE END POINT AS IT
HAS EVOLVED THROUGH
THE PAGES

WE BEGIN TO SEE MORE CLEARLY AN "END POINT" IN THE CHANGES THAT WE HAVE BEEN GOING THROUGH WITH OUR LEARNING PROCESS; AS WE PERCEIVE TIME TO APPEAR AS RELATIVE ITO THESE MATTERS AT THE HEART OF OUR BEING. THE ORTZELING EXPERIENCE OF MODIFYING THOUGHT AND LANGUAGE; WHILE CREATIVELY INVOLVING IDEAS TO SAY THE SAME THING THAT WE FEEL HELPS TO RELEASE SUPERFLUOUS BAGGAGE IN A WAY THAT MAKES PERFECT SENSE. IDEAS THAT WERE IN A STATE OF FLUX FOR YEARS PERHAPS

HAVE BEEN RESOLVED TO FORM THEIR CONTRIBUTION IN BRINGING CLOSURE TO CHAPTERS IN OUR LIVES.

WE CONTINUE TO ENJOY THE CREATIVE PROCESS IN THE FOLLOWING TEXT; THIS CONTAINS SERIES OF RAMBLING ORTZELS WITH THE DATES OF INCEPTION; THAT IS BEFORE THEIR COMPOSTING PROCESS AND COMPLETION. IN THE CASE OF THE MAJORITY OF ORTZELS IN THIS COLLECTION; THE ORIGINAL IS REPRESENTED HERE IN ITS FRESH PLUMAGE; WHILE SOME HAVE BEEN TRANSFORMED ENTIRELY INTO ANOTHER REALM OF THOUGHT FORM. THEY WILL CONTINUE TO EVOLVE IN ONE FORM OR ANOTHER; NO DOUBT, SO PLEASE ENJOY THIS SELECTION OF ORGELING ORTZELS.

YOURS,
PHYLO RAY

2010

12/01/10

YOU CAN TRY TAPPING THEM TO
BRING YOUR DREAMS TO
THE SURFACE

HIS LOVER DECIDED THAT
HE MUST DIE TO
WAIT FOR HER

CERTAIN THOUGHT FORMS ARE EVER
PRESENT IN THE
DOWSING MIND

MARRIAGE MIGHT PROPOSE ITSELF
DOWN THE ROAD IF
IT WORKS OUT

IS IT TIME THAT WE LEARN TO
CHOOSE TO FACE IT
IN THIS LIFE ?

THEY OPT TO LIVE LIKE THE BIRDS
IN THEIR FEATHERED
DIMENSION

WELCOME TO THE WORLD'S TOPMOST
MILITARY
FLASHPOINT MIND

ONE TRUE ACCOMPLISHMENT OF
OUR EXISTENCE
IS FORMLESS

HIS FATHER WAS THE GREATEST
GENERATION
HO HO HO

12/02/10

IFYOU HAVE WHAT YOU'VE WISHED FOR
WE MAY HAVE MISSED
THE MAIN POINT

WHAT MADE DINO SO UPSET
THERE WAS NO FREE
LUNCH THAT DAY

WHEN WE REPEAT OURSELVES WE
WANT TO HAVE MORE
CONFIDENCE

IT'S NOT THE WAY WE SAY IT
AS MUCH AS HOW
THEY LISTEN

THE MESSAGE OF THE FALL IS
THE HAIRY BEAST
TAKES THE BALL

12/03/10

THERE ARE MONSTERS ON THIS EARTH
AT EVERY TURN
THEY ARE US

JUST ANOTHER PREDATOR
WANDERING THRU
SO WHAT SUP ?

WHO NEEDS A PETTING ZOO FOR
SUPER WITCHES
KALI OM ?

JEALOUS GODS AND HUNGRY GHOSTS
TOGETHER THAT'S
ALL WE NEED

IT SERVES TO BE TRANSFORMING
WHEN LIFE BECOMES
AN ALLY

REVENGE IS NOT HELD TOO HIGH
ON THE GURU'S
LIST OF HITS

BUDDHA NEVER DID A THING
TO REJECT THIS
SUFFERING

MUSIC THAT WAS BELABORED
ROMANTICIZED
BORING SHLEP

IT'S ONLY YOUR DEVOTION
THAT SAVES US FROM
FANTASIES

LET'S GAZE AT THE STARS TONIGHT
COUNTING MORE THAN
WE'D HOPED FOR

12/04/10

THOR WAS UNHAPPY BECAUSE
HIS LEPRECHAUNS
HAD LEFT HOME

EARTH CHANGES SET THE RYTHM
SINCE THE TITANS
HAVE RETURNED

THE GAME THEY PLAY WITH EGO
BORDERS ON THE
RELATIVE

WHEN SOMEONE HAS BEEN CONDEMNED
PEOPLE TRY TO
FEEL SORRY

ARROGANT WITH CONCEIT YET
SURVIVING THEIR
OWN INTRIGUE ?

THE MAN OF KNOWLEDGE LOVES TO
EVOLVE BEYOND
SLAVERY

12/05/10

TO LAUGH AT OUR OWN PETTY
LIVES CONTEMPLATES
OUR WINNINGS

ENDINGS PROVIDE IMPETUS
FOR ALL TO FIND
BEGINNINGS

MILITARISTS FABRICATE
SOLDIERS PARADES
AND HEROES

COOKING SOME THING OFTEN HELPS
TO RELEASE THOSE
FREQUENT PANGS

IT'S REAL NICE TO FIND SOMEONE
TO CONDEMN YOU
FOR SUCCESS

THIS COLLECTION OF LOONIES
IS ALL YOU NEED
FOR OFFENSE

THE PRIDEFUL BUDDHA CANNOT
MAINTAIN PROPER
ATTUNEMENT

ALL THE PROPHETS AND SAINTS HAVE
TRANSMIGRATED
SOUL SUBSTANCE

12/06/10

PERHAPS WE DON'T UNDERSTAND
WHY THIS WORLD DOES
NOT EXIST

COLLECTING TOYS AT AGE THREE
APPREHENDED
CRIMINAL

THE SHAMAN WILL SAY TO YOU
WE JOURNEY TO
FIND YOUR SOUL

EVERYONE HAS THE RIGHT TO
WIN A SPECIAL
SACRIFICE

12/07/10

ANNIHILATION IS NAUGHT
WHILE ONE MAINTAINS
THEIR OWN SHIELD

LET US HAVE A TOAST FOR THE
PEOPLE WHO HUNT
AND A ROAST

THEY'RE QUITE FOND OF WOMEN WHO
PREFER TO HAVE
HUSBANDS STUFFED

12/08/10

HE HAS ALREADY STOLEN
ALL HE WANTED
WAS HIS SOUL

HONESTY IS THE SINCERE
FORM OF SELFLESS
REFLECTION

SELF PITY WAS HIS PRIME GAME
PAPARAZZI
HEAD HUNTER

EXCUSE US FOR WHAT WE'LL TAKE
TO APPEAR AS
A SHORT BREAK

LOOKING AT HIS LEGACY
DID NOT AMOUNT
TO THAT MUCH

THE ONLY BIG NEWS ON THE
DAY HE DIED HAD
CUT IT SHORT

ANYONE MIGHT HAVE POSSESSED
THAT INTIMATE
OPINION

QUITE AN ATTITUDE TO TAKE
ALL THE WAY FROM
HERE TO FORE

THE LOVE THEY LOST ERASED THEIR
ABILITY
TO SEE STRAIGHT

DID HE WANT TO BECOME A
MOGUL OR A
PEACENIK SAINT ?

OUR HEART IS LIKE A FLOWER
WE MUST KEEP IT
WELL WATERED

THEY SAY HE WAS AN ARTIST
FIRST AND FOREMOST
GAVE THAT UP

COMPOSED HIS MUSIC ATTACHED
FIRMLY TO THE
MIDDLE CLASS

THEY ADORED THE INTERNET
AND THE PHONY
PERSONA

DIED BEFORE HE GOT THERE DO
YOU THINK THEY MIGHT
LET HIM KNOW ?

HE ADMITS THAT HE WILL BE
RESPONSIVE TO
INDUCEMENT

WHEN THEY BROKE UP HE BECAME
A WATERED DOWN
SUBVERSION

HAVE NO IDEA WHAT THEY'RE
TALKING ABOUT
DON'T GO THERE

IT COMES AROUND TO THE POINT
HE WAS JUST A
CROWING COCK

EVERYONE WHO TALKS ABOUT
THEMSELVES SETS SOME
KIND OF TRAP

HE WOULD HAVE BEEN SEVENTY
FACING HIMSELF
TO GROW UP

OH YES HE WAS A DASHING
NARCISSISTIC
ANTI BLOKE

PINCHING MELODIES WAS HIS
ABILITY
AND PASSION

FALL OF THE AMERICAN
TYCOON USHERS
CONFUSION

TOO LATE TO ESCAPE FROM HERE
GOOD EXCUSE TAKE
A SHOWER

EVERYTHING IS OVER PRICED
HAS GOD EVER
OVER CHARGED ?

WHEN YOU FORGIVE ENEMIES
YOU ARE RELEASED
THAT 'S THE KEY

PERCEIVING THEM LIKE HE DID
HE NOW SEES WITH
STRANGER'S EYES

THOSE DOGS ARE OUT THERE BARKING
FOR THAT IS WHAT
THEY DO BEST

THE NEIGHBOR'S GONE FOR THE NIGHT
DOG LEFT OUTSIDE
LONELY BARK

SHE MADE IT BIG SERVING THOSE
RED CAVIAR
BULIMMIES

HER PAPA HAS COME ALONG
THE MONSTERS ARE
ON THE RUN

PLAY IT AGAIN UNTIL SHE
BECOMES THE CULT'S
FIGURINE

12/09/10

WHAT IS IT DISTINGUISHES
YOUR OUTLOOK FROM
THEIR VISTA ?

WITHOUT THE EGO'S PRESENCE
WE CAN TRULY
RULE HEAVEN

THERE IS NOTHING THAT CUTS THROUGH
KARMIC CRAP LIKE
THE MANTRA

12/10/10

WE TRY TO COME TO THE END
WHERE ALL WE FEEL
MEANS SOMETHING

DUE TO VARIOUS COMPLAINTS
BEST TO CONVERSE
HERBALLY

NO PROBLEM TAKING HIM DOWN
SIX SOUL PARTS LOST
IN NINE YEARS

THE ALCHEMY OF CARLOS
AND DON JUAN PROVED
MAGICAL

WE MIGHT AS WELL GO INTO
THAT GOOD NIGHT WITH
GREAT SPIRIT

12/10/10

BUDDHA'S LECTURES TAKE PLACE IN
DELUSIONAL
EARTHLY REALMS

WILL MEDITATION BRING YOU
ALL THE WAY TO
OUR DHARMA ?

THEY MIGHT FIND OUT THAT TO SERVE
IS ACTUALLY
IN CONTROL

YOU ARE IN LOVE BUT WHO KNOWS
HOW MANY OR
WHO WILL SHOW ?

THE WARTIME DISSEMBLEMENT
RALLY PRACTICE
BALMED HIM OUT

THE PRINCESS WANTS YOU TO PLAY
YOUR TUNES ON HER
BANDWAGON

TO MASTER TRANSMUTATION
CAN BE PLENTY
NOURISHING

TO BE COMPLETELY WELL LOVED
OH MERCY ME
BLESS MY SOUL

12/11/10

WHAT HE MEANT WAS THAT SHE WAS
SO SEDUCTIVE
THAT HE FLED

SHE SAID LET'S GET MARRIED NOW
AND TALK ABOUT
IT LATER

THERE'S NO PURPOSE ON THIS EARTH
ONLY ONE CAUSE
FOR TRIUMPH

THE DOG THAT BARKS SILENTLY
SUFFERS NO ONE
ANY FRIGHT

12/12/10

FAR BETTER TO DIE LAUGHING
THAN NOT TO HAVE
LAUGHED AT ALL

ALLURE ATTRACTED YOU TO
THAT FISHY WAY
OF THINKING

THERE IS NOTHING TO LIVE FOR
YET APPEARS AS
EVERYTHING

MUST BE THE FLOWERING JEANS
INFLUENCING
BEHAVIOR

GOD TRULY LOVES THOSE PEOPLE
EVEN THOUGH WE'RE
NOT INVOLVED

HE LET'S BEINGS COME IN AND
TAKE OVER THEN
THERE'S THE LAW

PREACHER KIND OF CHECKS THEM OUT
THEN THERE IS THE
MASS HEALING

AFTER A GOOD MANY LIVES
IT'S GOOD TO FIND
A GOOD TIME

HIS ANCESTORS DESIRED HIM
THE SORCERESS
CLAIMED HIM FIRST

IN PURSUIT OF PERFECTION
ONTO THE PATH
LESS TAKEN

12/14/10

LIFE DEVOURS ALL CONSCIOUSNESS
CATCHING PEOPLE
UNAWARE

OUR COSMOS MANIFESTS IN
THE SHAPE OF A
GLAZED DONUT

12/15/10

SOMETHIING WAS WRONG WITH THE MAN
OF NO DESIRE
THAT SHE FIXED

WHAT DID HE TELL THEM BEHIND
YOUR BACK IN FRONT
OF YOUR FACE ?

OUR WOUNDS HAVE HEALED WITH YOUR LOVE
WE BELIEVE IT
HAS HAPPENED

GIVE THEM ALL THE STRENGTH IN THE
UNIVERSE WITH
ASSURANCE

MEEK ORGANIZATIONS ARE
ALWAYS RIPE FOR
LEFT OVERS

THERE'S PLENTY OF LOVE IN THAT
DEPARTMENT HAVE
YOU FOUND SOME ?

FAST KARMA HAS A STRANGE WAY
OF DESTROYING
NORMALCY

YOU DID SAY THAT DREAMS EXIST
EVERYTHING IS
JUST A DREAM

GOLDEN WHITE LIGHT EMANATES
FROM THE HIGHEST
INTENTION

IS THERE NOTHING HELD SACRED
CAN WE REMAIN
IN THIS STATE ?

SOURCING THEM TENDS TO ASSUME
THE PERCEPTION
THAT WE LOVE

THEY'RE EXPECTING TO BECOME
VIRTUOUS IN
THEIR RELEASE

THEY AWAIT YOUR ANSWER WHILE
OUR QUESTIONING
PREPARES YOU

IN CHANTING THE HARMONIC
OM WE ATTRACT
THE BIRD TRIBE

MENDING TAKES ITS TIME TO GO
DOWN BEFORE IT
FEELS BETTER

CONFUSION AND COMPROMISE
OCCURS AROUND
CHRISTMAS TIME

MOURN FOR THE LIVES OF THE LOST
RETURN TO OUR
PLACE OF PEACE

THE MOON MUST BE FOLLOWING
THEIR TRAGEDY
IT'S QUITE SAD

HE GREW UP EATING CANDY
ACQUIRED A SWEET
BRAND OF LIFE

SELF PITY THEY NAILED TO THE
CROSS COULD NOT HAVE
SURVIVED LONG

CAN THE ROGUE NATION BRING ITS
DEMOCRACY
TO THE WORLD ?

SOME DISSIDENCE CREATED
THAT ARTISTIC
ENDEAVOR

IF YOU WANT TO HELP SOMEONE
CORRECTLY THEN
LEARN THYSELF

AVAILABILITY BOASTS TOLERANCE AND ACCEPTANCE

12/16/10

THAT BIRD IS ONE OF THOSE REAL
IMITATORS
IN THE FLOCK

COUPLE OF PINTS WITH PUMPKIN
CHEESECAKE GOOD TIME
TO BE GLAD

HIS BROTHER KICKED THE HABIT
NO ONE ELSE COULD
WEAR HIS BOOTS

ALTERED FATTER VERSIONS OF
MAD GENIUS SKIN
DOCTORS STINK

HE GREW UP TO BE SOMEONE
AND DOESN'T WANT
ANY THING

MASTERING SUCCESS IN LIFE
ADDS UP TO A
WHOLE LOT MORE

DIVINING FOR GREED NOT NEED
THEIR INTENT MAKES
LITTLE SENSE

ANGELS PAINTED ON THE WALLS
SURROUND THEIR ROOM
FLYING HIGH

FOUND OUT WHICH PEYOTE PLOT
HE WANTS TO BE
PLANTED IN ?

IT IS FEAR BASED CONSCIOUSNESS
WE HAVE TO CEASE
FEEDING ON

AIN'T NO SICK HEADS TIL YOU LOOK
AT THEM AND SAY
IT AIN'T ME

KALI L OVES YOU AND SWALLOWS
YOU HEAD FIRST WHEN
YOU DESIRE

LOOK AT THAT NECK SHE EXCLAIMS
COMPARING HIM
TO PRIZED DUCK

THEY WON'T SAY ANYTHING FOR
NOTHING SAYS IT
WELL ENOUGH

IT WORKS BY BRINGING IN THE
DIVAS TO HEAL
THE WHOLE EARTH

THEY WANT TO BE SAVED IN A
VERY SPECIAL
HOLY LAND

12/17/10

WE CERTAINLY CANNOT SEE
WHAT SHE HAS TRIED
TO MAINTAIN

THE COUNCILOR PROSECUTES
EVERYONE WITH
EQUAL CHARM

EGOS ARE MOST DANGEROUS
IN THE HANDS OF
NINCOMPOOPS

SHUCKS HE AIN'T PLAYING ANY
SILLY OLD GAME
THAT'S FUR SURE

THE EGO WILL NOT LET GO
UNLESS YOU CAN
FORGIVE IT

THE GRAND ZEN EXPERIENCE
PARODIES LIKE
FIASCOS

I KNOW WE'RE WRESTLING WITH IT
WHAT IS IT YOU
WANT TO SAY ?

12/18/10

DREAMS TRICK US INTO THINKING
WHAT WE'RE FEELING
CAN BE REAL

MALE PREDATORS FOCUS ON
WEAK WOMEN AND
PREJUDICE

TWIRLING SOMETHING CAN RESET
YOUR INNER SENSE
OF WARPED TIME

TEND TO COMPARE FAMILY
TO A NIGHTMARE
ALL DAY LONG ?

GONNA FIND MY LANDLORD A
ONE HORSE OPEN
SLEIGH TO RIDE

SHE WAS NOT GUILTY WITH HER
STOCKHOM SYNDROME
IT APPEARS

HE NEVER SPEAKS OF THEM SO
SEEMS LIKE THERE'S NONE
TO SPEAK OF

IS IT MOSTLY FEAR OF DEATH
DRIVES FOLKS TO HAVE
BAMBINOS ?

EVEN WITHOUT A NICKNAME
HE IS STILL IN
THEIR PRAYERS

12/19/10

CHANTING SOUNDS MOST BEAUTEOUS
THE ENTIRE HOST
ANGELIC

SONGSTER REVEALS A CROCK OF
HOKEY POKEY
DING A LINGS

SO THOROUGHLY AFFRONTED
FORCED TO BECOME
THEIR LEADER

WHEN IT COMES TO WRITING YOU
NEVER REST ON
YOUR LABELS

IT IS THEIR OWN SANITY
THE HEALERS SOON
RECOGNIZE

ALL ROADS LEAD US HOME BUT THEN
YOU MIGHT WANT TO
FIND A PATH

YOU KNOW THAT SIDE IS BETTER
THAN THIS ONE AND
THE OTHER

IT'S NOT WHAT YOU SAY TO THEM
IT'S HOW YOU SPEAK
IT TO THEM

IT WAS THEIR TRAP THAT CAME BACK
CAUGHT THEM IN ITS
MIGHTY JAWS

THESE ORTZELS AREN'T VERY MUCH
TURNS OUT THEY ARE
JUST ENOUGH

SHE'S SO CALM AND COLLECTED
UNTIL SHE TEARS
YOUR HEART OUT

NEVER SEEN ANY CRITTERS
EVER LOOK LIKE
THAT ONE COULD

COME UPON THEIR SWEET RIDE HOME
WE SHALL LOVE THEM
EVER MORE

JOYOUS TIMES TO SING WHEN THEY
FIND THEMSELF NEAR
THE NEW YEARS

SEEMS TO ME YOU GOT TO PLAY
THE FOOL TO ACT
LIKE THAT WAY

THERE'S NO CHAINS ON THE LONESOME
ONLY GOOD TIMES
TO BE WON

THE BOOK WRITTEN FOR DOG ZEN
CHEWS THE FAT IN
BONE HEAVEN

FREE TO GO HIS WAY HE MIGHT
HAVE HAD TO BREAK
THE OLD MOLD

FIRST HE OUGHT TO GET RID OF
SOME OF THEM AND
FREE THE REST

LIABLE TO BE LAUDED IN
PUBLIC YET CURSED
IN PRIVATE

SET OFF AS FAST AS HE COULD
GO BUT COULD NOT
PART WITH THEM

WE NEVER MET A YOGI
WHO WAS A STICK
IN THE MUD

THERE WAS ONLY ONE BUDDHA
THE ONE WHOM YOU
RAN INTO

WAVE FORMS THAT DON'T END CAN GO
ON FOREVER
LIKE WE DO

HE HAS GIVEN HIS LIFE TO
THIS WORK AND CAN
MOVE ON NOW

IF WE STAY TOO LONG IN THIS
ONE SPOT WE MIGHT
LOSE IT ALL

IT DOESN'T INVOLVE ALL THAT
GIBBERISH TO
GAIN FREEDOM

IF YOU LET IT GO ITS COURSE
SOON ENOUGH IT
LETS YOU BE

HE OFTEN WONDERED IF THE
INTROSPECTION
WAS BIASED

AN OBSESSIVE COMPULSIVE
DISORDER CAN
GO LIKE THIS

SPIRITUAL ONE UPMANSHIP
CAN'T BRING US TO
PERFECTION

THE MENTOR SAYS BECOME ONE
WITH IT AND THEN
HEAL THY SELF

WISE WOMAN CIRCLES THE SEED
THAT'S TO BE SHARED
WITH THE LIGHT

THE EARTH WILL PERISH BEFORE
THEY HURT A HAIR
ON HIS HEAD

SHE CAN'T STEAL ANY MORE SOUL
IT'S ALL THE SOUL
THAT HE HAD

ALL THAT ABUSE OF POWER
IS FINE WITH HIGH
INTEREST

THE TWO FACES OF EVE CAN
ACTUALLY SPIN
ROUND AND ROUND

IT'S NOT WHERE THEY ARE IN THE
DREAM BUT WHERE THEY'RE
COMING FROM

SHE BELIEVES THAT SHE CAN SHARE
HER CAKE AND EAT
IT AS WELL

BIRD RATTLES MIGHT HAVE SAVED THEM
BUT THEY WOULD NOT
HEAR OF IT

THE ORTZELS WERE KILLNG HIM
AND DO YOU THINK
THEY COULD STOP ?

IT MIGHT SMELL GOOD IF HE WOULD
COMPOSE TIME TO
CHANGE HIS CLOTHES

12/20/10

SILENT RESPONSE CAN BE MORE
TO THE POINT THAN
QUICK RETORT

THERE'S PRETTY MUCH OF NOTHING
BETWEEN ATOMS
NO MATTER

WANTING TO GET TO KNOW YOU
THEY'VE BEFRIENDED
YOUR DOUBLE

THE FLOWER GENERATION
MADE A BOUQUET
WITH THEIR THING

12/21/10

AS LONG AS MARIJUANA
GUIDES HIS JUDGEMENT
HE'S ENSLAVED

MOTHER PREPARES FOR THE BUN
IN THE BASKET
SO WHOOPY

DEAR SIBLINGS SEASON'S GREETINGS
WHY NOT GET SO
PERSONAL

HERE ARE A COUPLE OF SOAPS
AND ONE VERMONT
POTPOURI

PERHAPS THOSE CANADIAN
GOATS CAN REALLY
GO FLYING

THEY LOOK LIKE FLYING SHEEP WITH
BOTH EARS STICKING
STRAIGHT OUT FLAT

THANKS TO HOSPITALITY
WITH UNDYING
INTEREST

FAITH IN LIFE CONNECTING FAITH
THROUGH LIFETIME GOALS
WHAT THE HEY

BEING A MAN HE CAN DO
WHAT HIS CONSCIENCE
DEVISES

SPURN THE WITCH WHO PLUNDERS THUS
MAKING IDOLS
OF FALSE GODS

BY DEFINITION THESE ARE
COMPLEXITIES
SIMPLIFIED

IS THERE A COURSE TO DISCLAIM
ANONYMOUS
EXPOSURE ?

PLAYING THE GAME YOU NOW KNOW
WHERE BUDDHA'S THOUGHTS
CAN BE FOUND

EVEN IF IT'S A LITTLE
TIP OR SOMETHING
HE LEAVES IT

HE WEARS IT TO LET YOU KNOW
THAT ONCE HE HAD
A MOTHER

THEY AWOKE TWO DAYS LATER
HAVING SURVIVED
CHILDREN'S DAY

YOU HEARD ABOUT THE CRAZY
RUMORS DON'T TRUST
SISSY GOON ?

SHE WOULD LIKE TO ENLIGHTEN
EVERYONE FOR
GOOD MEASURE

LOOK AT YOU A REAL BEAUTY
BEYOND ANY
CONCEPTION

TO LIVE WITHOUT DREAMING IS
CONTRARY TO
LIFE ITSELF

HE DOESN'T LIVE ANYWHERE
DUE TO THE FACT
HE'S NOT THERE

BY SEEING WITH OUR HEART SENSE
WE OPEN WITH
DIVINE SENSE

12/23/10

ARE WE SO WELL TRAINED WITH THE
EXPECTATIONS
OF A DOG ?

REGENERATIVE TEA BLEND
FORMULA FOR
PURGATION

A BODY MADE OF LIGHT IT
IS MUCH TO BE
EMPHASIZED

HE DOESN'T KNOW WHERE HE'S FROM
DO YOU THINK THEY
CARE THAT MUCH ?

IF LITTLE GERMS CAN DO THAT
WE'RE NOT READY
FOR THIS ONE

TO PAINT ON THOSE CHAIRS WOULD BE
SACRILEGE THEY'RE
DE MEUBLES

IT'S YOUR IMAGINATION
THAT REQUIRES SOME
MAINTAINANCE

AMERICANA DREAMING
NAIVETE~
PERSONA

INDULGING IN DREAMS CAN BE
USEFUL AS A
PROFESSION

CELEBRATING TO FIND YOUR
WAY IS EASY
WHEN CHOSEN

12/24/10

IN REGARDS TO OUR BLESSING
SO MUCH HAS BEEN
ACCOMPLISHED

HOW DOES IT GO WISE WOMAN
HAS EVERYTHING
BEEN RESTORED ?

SHE DEMANDS TO BE SEDUCED
BY ILLUSION'S
FANTASIES

THEY FELL INTO THEIR LITTLE
TRAP THAT IS THEIR
TRAPOLIE

SIT AND HEAL NO THIS IS NOT
ADVERTISING
FOR YOUR DOG

IT WAS IN THE BELLY OF
A CROCODILE
FOUND HIS FAME

YOU DON'T KNOW ANYBODY
MIGHT NEED A NEW
GONG TO STRIKE ?

SEASONS GREETINGS FOR ALL IN
OUR VERY BEST
INTEREST

NOBODY MADE HEAVEN THIS
TIME AROUND SO
DON'T WORRY

12/25/10

EVERYONE MIGHT LIKE TO HAVE
THE ATTACHMENTS
TO THEIR SOUL

TRY TALKING NORMAL TO YOUR
BEST FRIEND THAT IS
SHEER NONSENSE

HEAVENLY HE MUST HAVE BEEN BORN
WITH A JESUS
HOROSCOPE

WHAT WE WANT TO DO IS TO
FIND US A BAG
OF ORTZELS

IT READS PLEASE ASK IN ORDER
TO RECEIVE WHAT
YOU CAN GIVE

IS IT CALLED THE CILANTRO
RECONNECTION
WITH GARLIC

CERTAIN FIXER UPPERS ARE
REMARKABLY
LUCRATIVE

PLEASE BEWARE HOW THEY PREFER
TO BE PLACED ON
PEDESTALS

FOR WE MUST BEGIN SOMEWHERE
TO RECOGNIZE
THE GODSEND

ALL THESE MERRY CHRISTMASES
SUCH A DELIGHT
FOR HEART STRINGS

THOSE THINGS DON'T LAST FOREVER
'SPECIALLY THE DOG
CHEWS ON 'EM

ANGELS SEE A DIFFERENT
WORLD THAN THE ONE
APPEARS HERE

DISCONTINUITY OF
AWARENESS TAKES
PRISONERS

SITS NEAR THE EDGE OF THE BENCH
FEELING A BIT
NUDGY LIKE

ZEN DOG MILLIONAIRES IS WHAT
THEY WANT TO MAKE
OUT OF IT

12/26/10

WHO'S YOUR LATEST BOOGY MAN
MIGHT THEY BE OUR
BOGUS FRIEND ?

SAINTS ARE FOUND IN SOLITUDE
ENVISIONING
PURE NEW LIFE

WOULDN'T WANT TO CONTRIBUTE
WHAT PROVES COUNTER
CONDUCIVE

THE PORTAL OF THE SAINT DOES
RECEIVE AND SEND
SILENT LOVE

IT'S TRAP AFTER TRAP AFTER
BOTTOMLESS PIT
EXTRICATE

IT IS ONLY THOSE THINGS THAT
ARE ETERNAL
EXIST HERE

THERE ARE SOME NEW FOUND FREEDOMS TO
TO REACT TO
FOR PETE'S SAKE?

YOU DON'T EVER WANT TO SAY
TO BIMBO DREAMS
DON'T EXIST

SHE ALWAYS MANAGED TO TRICK
BOYS TO BEAT UP
EACH OTHER

THOSE GENTLEMEN DOWSERS WEAR
WHITE SLACKS AND SIT
IN LAWN CHAIRS

YOU HAVE YOUR TICKET FOR THE
WITCH HUNT TODAY
OH GOODY

THEY HAVE BEEN MOST TRAGICALLY
COMPUTERIZED
UPDATED

THE SECRET RESTS WITH THE ONES
WHO DON'T HAVE TO
RETURN HERE

UNIVERSAL LOVE IS A
POTENT IMPETUS
TO AFFIRM

SHE WAS TOTALLY HOOKED ON
INTELLECTUAL
BANDER SNATCH

WHAT IS PREZ GONNA DO NOW
SIT ON THE THRONE
AND JUST DIE ?

THEY DISCOVERED HIS NAME WAS
SEPPI GOVIN
LATE IN LIFE

NEVER BE BORED MY DAR LINK
THESE ARE TIMES TO
CONNECT WITH

DEVOTION CAN BE INTENSE
ESPECIALLY
HAVING FUN

YOUR COMPUTER MIND WILL TEND
TO DEVOUR THE
HUMAN MIND

HIS BOSS MADE HIM CRAZY HE
WAS LUCKY TO
WALK AWAY

THE ROAD LESS TAKEN LEADS TO
THE UNKNOWN PATH
OF THE HEART

THE FAMILY CURSE KEPT HER
IN ITS LIFE LONG
CRUSHING GRIP

LACKING SEPARATION THEY
HOLD THE PROMISE
OF HEALING

THERE IS NO PAIN ON THIS EARTH
IF THE MIND IS
PARADISE

KIND OF MAKES YOU STOP TO THINK
THAT WE HAVE NOT
THOUGHT TOO MUCH

SWEET LOVE SAYS OUR SOUL MOMMA'S
GONNA HAVE HER
PEACE OF PIE

SURPRISINGLY THE BODY
IS NOT VERY
MUCH ATTACHED

IS TRUTH YOUR SWEET LITTLE THING
PLAYING NO REAL
ROLE IN LIFE ?

THEIR DISEASE COULD PART THEM FROM
THEIR CREATOR
OR SAVE THEM

HE WAS BEING KIDNAPPED AS
HIS GUILT BEGAN
TO LEAVE HIM

THERE IS A WAY AROUND IT
TO OUTFLANK THEIR
SURROUND SOUND

TRY OUT THIS SOAP TO FIND IF
YOU'RE SLIPPERY
WHEN ALL WET

2011

1/01/11

DID HE EVER WONDER IF
GOD WERE COMPLETE
WITHOUT HIM ?

YOU KNOW SOMETHING'S UP WHEN THEY
MAINTAIN CHRIST'S THREE
ALIENS

TRY NOT TO FEEL THREATENED BY
ANOTHER'S FRANK
AWARENESS

THIS IS YOUR TOTALITY
HOLY DIVA'S
HOT SPICED CHAI

THAT WAS THE MOST BOOTY FULL
COMPOSTED POEM
EVER POOMED

HE DOESN'T HAVE TO PICK UP
STARS HE STORES THEM
IN HIS HEAD

SATSANG TIME IS FOR THE BEST
PSEUDI BUDDHI
BEHAVIOR

THOSE FAMOUS POLITICIANS
MADE EVERYTHING
AN EVENT

ONLY ONE KINGDOM THAT'S NOT
GOD FORSAKEN
ELIZ BETH

LIFE'S EXTREME MY GOODNESS BUT
YOU REMAINED TOO
UNDAUNTED

THEY ARE TOO SMART IT'S NOT WORTH
TALKING ABOUT
NORMALCY

SOME DAY WE'LL LEARN TO FORGIVE
OUR TRESPASSERS
AND DEBTORS

YOU WILL FIND THERE IS NO ONE
HERE AND NO PLACE
TO HIDE OUT

YOGIS ATTAIN FREEDOM WHEN
THEIR REM SLEEP CHARTS
ARE MAINTAINED

1/03/11

THEY SAY HE CAN TALK REAL GOOD
CAUSE HE'S GOT THE
GIFT OF GAB

THE VICIOUS WITCH WAS OF GREAT
NECESSITY
TO HER WORK

SHE'D MADE IT PLAIN THAT SHE OWNED
THE SOUL OF HER
FAMILY

1/04/11

SHE ATTAINED SNOW WHITE STATUS
WHEN THEY GAVE HER
PORCHE AWAY

THERE'S NO WAY THAT HE CAN SEE
THE FOREST IN
THAT SUNSET

GIVING ANYTHING AWAY
IS A PROBLEM
FOR BABOONS

THE CAT KNOWS IT'S FORTUNATE
INDEED TO SEE
IN THE DARK

1/05/11

FREE THE MIND FROM COMMOTION
WITH LOVE AND JOY
FILL IT UP

JOY'S GOOD BUT AMBITION IS
BAD SO THAT'S THE
STORY FOLKS

CAN WE LOVE OTHERS ONLY
THROUGH THE GRACE OF
THEIR SAVIOUR ?

MANIFESTATIONS OF GRACE
ARE EXQUISITE
EMOTIONS

THINK ABOUT TAKING A BREAK
FOR YOUR MONARCH
ROYALLY

WELCOME DEATH THEN ENJOY YOUR
LIFE UNTO THE
MAXIMUM

DON'T FORGET TO SAY YOUR GRACE
FOR THAT IS THE
REAL BLESSING

1/06/11

IT'S ORTZELS' RAMBLING PROCEEDS
TO UNDO THIS
UNIVERSE

THEIR SACRED MUSIC IS WHAT
SUSTAINS THEM THROUGH
THE LONG NIGHT

UNLIKE MINDS OFTEN FIT QUITE
JOINTLY WITHIN
NOVELTY

HE DABBLED IN ORGELING
ORTZELS THEN SHE
DISPATCHED HIM

1/07/11

THE THREE POISONS ARE NOTHING
WHEN COMPARED WITH
EMPTINESS

WHO WAS IT WHO SAID THAT ONE
MUST STRIVE TO EAT
DIVINE LOVE ?

MULTI TASKING INTERPLAY
WITH LIGHT REVEALS
ALL THE HOOKS

RECEIVING SUPPORT FROM HER
FOLLOWERS SHE
AVOIDS THEM

THE SIGN READS ARBITRARY
GOVERNMENT BASED
COUNSELING

1/08/11

BECOMING TOO POWERFUL
THEY FELL FOR THAT
HAREBRAINED TRICK

FEELING SORRY FOR OURSELVES
ONLY BRINGS US
BACK AGAIN

LAUGHING OUT LOUD MAKES THEM WANT
TO LAUGH OUT LOUD
MUCH LOUDER

1/09/11

MUST WE ACCOMPLISH ANGUISH
BEFORE WE TRY
OUT OUR WISH ?

IT'S THROUGH AN UNLIKELY SOURCE
PEOPLE MAINTAIN
INNER PEACE

THE SUN DOES NOT BOTHER US
ALL WINTER LONG
IN THIS TOWN

CAN'T WE FOLLOW THE ACTION
IT'S NOT GOING
ANYWHERE ?

PERHAPS WE'LL BE THAT LONELY
UNTIL WE MOVE
OUT OF HERE

IMMERSION IS THE KEY TO
RELATIONSHIPS
FOREVER

THEY'RE NOT BORED AT ALL WITH THE
REVOLUTION
IT'S THEIR YOUTH

TAKE ONE LITTLE BABY STEP
ASIDE AND WE
MIGHT VANISH

YOU GOT THAT MUCH IN THE BANK
READY TO BURN
MAKE SOME SMOKE

BY SINKING FANGS INTO FRIENDS
VAMPIRES SHARECROP
THEIR VICTIMS

1/10/11

TELL THE HEAVIES IN YOUR DREAM
TO BEGIN TO
LIGHTEN UP

LOSERS CAN CONQUER ONLY
WHEN THEY ASCEND
SOMEWHERE ELSE

YOU DON'T WANT ANY BODIES
TO FEEL LIKE THEY
MIGHT OWN YOU

IS IT NECESSARY TO
REKINDLE OLD
FLAMES FOR WARMTH ?

NEXT THEY TRY TO ENSNARE YOU
TEACH THEM TO BE
YOUR CLOSE FRIEND

MOJO GOT HIS CHARM FROM YOUR
REP BUT WOULD HE
TAKE THE RAP ?

SOME WOMEN LIKE TO FEEL THEY
CAN GET PREGNANT
TO SOLVE THINGS

WAS THE DISTANT PAST CONFUSED
ABOUT WHAT'S IN
THE PRESENT ?

AN OPTIMIST'S TRUE LOVE IS
AROUND EVERY
BLIND CORNER

IT'S OLD WOMEN WHO GIVE YOU
THE TIME OF DAY
DON'T ASK WHY

DOYLE'S JUNGLE WAS QUITE A
FREAKY WORLD TO
STUMBLE ON

THERE ARE NONE TO JUDGE THE SANE
THEY ARE RARELY
EVER FOUND

WILDCRAFTING ORTZELS MEANS THAT
YOU JOURNEY 'TIL
THEY FIND YOU

OUR UNDYING INTEREST
IN YOUR FUTURE
BEGINS NOW

WORKING AT SOMETHING BRAINLESS
'TWAS ABLE TO
MAKE ENDS MEET

THEIR DESCENT TO THE BOTTOM
REVELLED ON THE
RED CRAB'S SHELL

IT IS BUT THE FINEST LOVE
GUIDES US INTO
THIS QUANDRY

HE'S BETTER OFF PLAYING THE
FOOL THAN THAT DARNED
DILLETANTE

DOES IT MATTER HOW LONG IT
TAKES US BREAKING
THIS NEW GROUND ?

TO WRITE LIKE THAT YOU'LL END UP
DRAMATICALLY
STUPENDOUS

THEY'VE TRIED EVERY TRICK TO GET
BETWEEN HIM AND
HIS SOUL MATE

AWAKENINGS RELEASE THAT
KIND OF HEAVY
COMMITTMENT

1/11/11

DID YOU FIND YOUR CRYSTAL SKULL
IN THE REMOTE
WILDERNESS ?

CREATING JOY QUIETS THE
MIND SO THEY CHOOSE
SUFFERING ?

HARDLY FOUND ANYTHING IN
THIS WORLD BETTER
SAID THAN DONE

TAKING CONTROL OF OTHERS
REGARDLESS OF
WHO THEY ARE ?

MEDITATE BEYOND THE VOID
LOCATE OUR OM
ENERGY

PAST LIFE MEMORY REGAINED
CONTENTMENT BRINGS
COMMITMENT

OF ALL THE THOUGHTS CONSIDERED
CONTEMPLATION
ACTIVATES

WHY KEEP WATCHING THAT FILM NOIR
EMULATING
AFFLICTION ?

1/13/11

THE VICTIM OF STALKING WAS
QUESTIONED AND GUILT
PROJECTED

DAT OBTUSE PLATITUDE IST
DIDACTIC MIT
SAPPY SHLUSH

INCLUSIVE VEHICLES
CAN ENLIVEN
YOUR LANGUAGE

THEIR CATAMOUNT PROVED TO BE
ALTOGETHER
INTRIGUING

NONSENSE IS THE BIG GAME OF
THIS INTELLECT'S
HOT PURSUIT

THE DEMON CRIED OUT OH LORD
PLEASE PROTECT US
FROM FREEDOM

THERE'S LOTS OF INFORMATION
AND WITHOUT A
DOUBT KNOWLEDGE

IF ONLY A THOUGHT REMAINS
MIGHT AS WELL BE
A GOOD ONE

IT CAN BE SHOCKING TO FIND
FOREVER'S MORE
OF THE SAME

ALL THEY REALLY WANT IS YOU
THEN THEY'LL TELL YOU
WHAT TO DO

1/14/11

WE ARE GOING SOME PLACE WHEN
IT'S OUR DRUTHERS
TAKES US THERE

EXPECTATIONS HAVE GRANTED
THEIR CORRUPTING
CONDITION

THERE ARE TRAGEDIES OUT THERE
BUT NOT FOR THE
BLUE GURU

MAINTAIN YOUR BOOTY CUTIE
LEVITATION
IS THE CUE

SWEETIE MAKES YOUR LOVING RHYME
YOU CHOOSE TO BE
HOME ON TIME

IT IS CALLED AIR CONDITIONED
THIS COOL KIND OF
SURRENDER

EGO NEVER SETS US FREE
WE'RE ONLY LED
TO BELIEVE

HAVE YOU HEARD WE ARE RELEASED
WHEN WE CAN CHOOSE
TO BE FREE ?

NO ONE IS EVER SAFE HERE
WHEN EGO MAKES
ALL THE RULES

THEY MIGHT HAVE HER LOOK LIKE THAT
SHE'D RATHER BE
LIKE HERSELF

ARE YOU REALLY SOMEBODY
OR ARE THEY JUST
NOBODIES

HE HAS NEVER BEEN BULLIED
BECAUSE HE DOES
NOT GO THERE

OH DIVINE ONE HOW DO YOU
KNOW WHAT'S TRULY
GOOD FOR YOU ?

IT WAS A GOOD TIME TO LEAVE
JUST BEFORE THE
MASSACRE

1/15/11

THE SIGN THAT READS LOST SOULS FOUND
FAILED TO NOTICE
THEY'RE FOR SALE

NEVER AT A LOSS FOR WORDS
HE'S GOT NOTHING
LEFT TO LOSE

HEY LOOP DE LOO WAKE UP NOW
TIME'S A FLYING
START SAILING

WE'VE MET SOME CREATURES LIKE THAT
THE FLAUNTILY
KINGDOM BOUND

NOTHING LIKE DOUBLE LOBSTER
TO WARM COCKLES
OF THE HEART

WE DIDN'T THINK ABOUT THOSE
CONSEQUENCES
DON'T EXIST

HIDDEN DETAILS OF YOUR LIFE
POSE WHAT KIND OF
A QUESTION ?

THOSE WERE MORE THAN CONUNDRUMS
ANOMALOUS
AND BLATANT

MUST BE KIND OF REALLY BAD
PEOPLE BELIEVE
IN EVIL

WE'LL BE ALL RIGHT FOR A WHILE
NO SOLUTION
IS FOOL PROOF

HOLY SPIRIT USES THAT
ILLUSION TO
SET US FREE

WE WOULD LIKE TO FIND OUR WAY
HOME AGAIN IN
THIS LIFETIME

ONE INSPIRED IDEA SAYS
THAT WE CAN BE
DIFFERENT

TRUE FORGIVENESS CAN REALLY
BE THE GREATEST
HAND ME DOWN

SOMETHING ABOUT VIBRATIONS
SAYS ALIENS
FOUND THIS WORLD

ENERGY COMES FROM OUR THOUGHTS
BUT THAT IS NOT
ALL WE HAVE

IT WAS A GREAT MEAL PAID FOR
WITH EVERY LAST
BITE OF IT

NOT EVEN THE BLEEDING HEARTS
COULD POSSIBLY
BRING HIM DOWN

HIS PARENTS WORRIED ABOUT
BAILING HIM OUT
LOOK AT THEM

YOUR SPECIAL LITTLE HOLY
SENTIENT BEINGS
HAVE BEEN SAVED

THEY SUSPECT THERE IS SOMETHING
TO FIND STUCK HERE
IN THE MUD

IT'S SUPPOSED TO BE THE MUSE
COMPOSES THOSE
SUPER RIFFS

THEY DON'T WISH TO APE THESE TRAPS
MERELY USING
BANANNAS

IDEAS BEGIN TO FORM
AS SOON AS THEY
HAVE THE WORD

1/17/11

THESE ARE HELPING US TO SCULPT
WHAT THEY CALL OUR
MENTAL BLOCKS

IN YOUR HEART THERE CERTAINLY
ARE MOMENTS OF
CONTENTMENT

IS THERE NO PLACE TO GO WHERE
YOU CAN HANG OUT
TO BE FOUND ?

SPIDER WEBS SPUN THROUGHOUT THIS
ENTIRE STAR EYED
UNIVERSE

THERE IS SOME ACTUAL LAUGHTER
TO BE FOUND OUT
IT'S FAR OUT

HIS FAMILY UPBRINGING
ACCOMPLISHED TRUE
DETACHMENT

THE GOAL OF TRUE LOVE CAN BE
TO GET A GRIP
ON ONE SELF

HOW DID THEY EVER FIND IT
IN THE PEACH JAM
SPREAD LIKE THAT ?

HARDLY INDIFFERENT PERCIEVING
THE FAILURE TO
MEDIATE

THAT LITTLE FROG THEERE IS A
SYMBOL FOR OUR
FERTILE TEA

THE ECOSYSTEM IS GONE
SO THEY HAVE THEIR
PARKING LOT

TOULOUSE LAUTREC MAKES PRETTY
BALMY SORTS OF
IMPRESSIONS

ONE OF THOSE THOUGHTS CAN PROCEED
TO UNDO THIS
ENTIRE WORLD

THAT FORMULA WON'T SUCCEED
IN SOLVING THEIR
DILEMMA

HER SOUL HAS BEEN SENT SOMEWHERE
IT CAN BEGIN
TO SURVIVE

THAT BIMONTHLY POETRY
SLASH AND BURN MADE
PERFECT SENSE

POEMS COMPOSED IN SUCH A
WAY AS TO BE
PERFECT PROSE

VERSIFIED MIND SET MAY SERVE
TO INCREASE THEIR
ASSEMBLAGE

HE WILL NEVER HAVE THE KEYS
TO UNLOCK THIS
UNIVERSE ?

OH YES HE'S CRACKED EVERY
KOAN SWEET LITTLE
CRAZED CONE HEAD

WAS IT LAO TZU WHO ONCE ASKED
WOULDN'T IT BE
NICE TO BE ?

DISSEMBLANCE TURNS OUT TO POSE
SOLUTIONS FOR
ENJOINMENT

WHY JUMP TO A CONCLUSION
WHEN WE CAN TAKE
LEAPS OF FAITH

HELLO HELLO HEY THERE IS
NO ONE HERE BUT
WHERE WERE YOU ?

IS THERE NO ONE ELSE WHO CAN
DOWSE YOUR MENTAL
LOCATION ?

HE WANTED TO VERBALIZE
BUT WAITED FOR
THOUGHTS TO COME

THERE IS NO KNOWLEDGE IN LIFE
BETTER THAN A
CLEAR CONSCIENCE

THE WAY TO COMPOSE POEMS
IS TO WRITE A
BUNCH OF THEM

IT BEATS ME HOW THEY CAN SAY
ETERNAL BLISS
IS SILENT

I LOVE YOU MOTHERLY MOON
AND ALL THE STARS
SO FAR OUT

LIVING IN THIS ALIEN
ENVIRONMENT
STILLS THE MIND

WE BECOME GOOD BUDDHISTS WHEN
WE TRULY LOVE
ALL OUR SELVES

THEY PROBABLY JUST WANT TO
SAY WHAT YOU MEAN
AND WHAT NOT

UPRISINGS HAPPEN BUT IT'S
BEST TO LET THEM
DO THEIR TIME

THIS EXERCISE HELPS YOU TO
CLARIFY AND
DRAIN THE MIND

IT TAKES INVESTIGATION
TO REMOVE ALL
OBSTACLES

ORIGINAL NATURE IN
CREATURES IS MOST
DELIGHTFUL

NO ONE IS OUT TONIGHT AT
MINUS TWO TURN
OUT THE LIGHT

THE POWERS THAT BE DO EXIST
SOMEWHERE BEYOND
THIS PLANET

AFTER HE WAS CREMATED
SHE SPOKE ABOUT
HER OLD FLAME

WHY DON'T WE REMOVE IT BY
WORKING ON THE
INFARCTION ?

BE A GOOD BUDDHIST AND DON'T
GO OUT THERE TO
MEET BUDDHA

SHE'S SOME KIND OF CHEWBACCA
PRINCESS JUST LIKE
HER MAW WAS

SORRY BUT YOUR ID IS TOO
VAST FOR ORTZEL'S
TEENSY BRAIN

SHE SMILES LIKE THAT BECAUSE SHE
DOESN'T CARE TO
DO MUCH ELSE

YOU SAY ALL YOU WANT IS SOME
SWEET FREEDOM TO
LIBERATE

KIND OF DISAPPEARED FROM THIS
WORLD DID YOU GET
THEIR ADDRESS ?

THAT DRAMATICALLY ALTERED
JUSTICE INDUCED
FAIR TRAUMA

HEAR MICE IN THE CEILING THEN
THE DOOR BEGINS
ITS SQUEEKING

NO MATTER WHAT THE WEATHER
GOD BLESS THE MILK
YOU MOO COW

OPENING ORTZEL DOORWAYS
CONTEMPLATION
IS THE KEY

THEY CAN HELP US OUT OF HERE
REALITY'S
ON ITS WAY

WHY NOT BECOME ENLIGHTENED
STOP BEHAVING
LIKE THE SCLAVE

AT TWELVE ABOVE ZERO OUR
SNOW SUBLIMATES
IN THE SUN

1/18/11

SORRY THEY CAN'T FIND ANY
JEALOUSY BASED
ON THAT GREED

COMPOSED YOUR DIARY TO
ADD A LITTLE
FLAVORING ?

IT WAS MAD THE WAY SHE LAUGHED
COULD NOT GO THERE
WERE SO CLOSE

TIPPED OFF FROM THE VERY START
MUST HAVE BEEN THE
LIP SERVICE

CANNOT BEGIN TO SURVIVE
THIS CLIMATE WITH
NO PLECTRUM

THAT THING ABOUT HIM SHE MADE
IT ALL UP IN
HER BELLY

JUST LIKE ANY WORK OF OUGHT
QUALITY IS
COMPOUNDED

SUPPOSE WE SEE BEGINNINGS
BEFORE WE COME
TO THE END ?

WE LOVED YOUR PERCEPTION YOU
SWEET LIL' COMPLEX
GOING DOWN ?

DON'T GET MATERIALIZED
AND LOSE YOUR FAITH
ENTIRELY

THE OPENING HEART CREATES
GREAT DESIRE FOR
BLISSFUL LOVE

COURAGE IS WAITING FOR US
PATIENTLY THERE
WITHIN RANGE

HOW IS LITTLE DAKINI
DOING IS SHE
CUTE AND SWEET ?

LIFE IS WORTH EVERYTHING AND
EVERYBODY
PAYS SOMETHING

IT'S ALL GREEK TO THEM WHEN WE
SPEAK PARA POEM
DOKIAN

DOWN TO EARTH BULLROAR ACTS LIKE
LIKE LOONY TOON
POSSESSION

AH HA HA HA HO HO HO
WOOF WOOF WOOFY
WOOFY WOOF

LITTLE HOLIES PLAYING GOD
HELP US OUT PART
OF THE WAY

1/20/11

WE CAN WORK LIKE DOGS AND WIND
UP WHERE WE OUGHT
TO BEGIN

EACH TIME WE THOUGHT ABOUT THAT
OUR TRAIN OF THOUGHT
WAS DERAILED

THEY'RE DYING TO BEGIN TO
LIVE THE COURSE IN
MIRACLES

NEW AGE OF INFORMATION
HAILS COLLUSION'S
INVASION

THEY DISAGREE ABOUT WHAT
TENDS TO BE IN
AGREEMENT

BETTER TO BE ECSTATIC
THAN TO FIND YOU'VE
BEEN OBSESSED

YOUR DESIRE FOR SUCCESS GOES
HAND IN HAND WITH OUR
EXERTION

LOVE OFFERS ENERGY FOR
YOUR DIVINELY
INSPIRED WORK

JESUS IS WELL AND HE LOVES
WITH US TODAY
SAY AMEN

HALLELUJAH PRAISE THE LORD
IT'S NOT ONLY
ON SUNDAYS

THE SUN IS SHINING AND YET
SNOW FLAKES ARE STILL
COMING DOWN

EVALUATIONS MISTAKE
PEOPLE FOR WHAT
THEY ARE NOT

AND NOW WE'RE GONNA DRIVE THIS
STUPID LITTLE
DINKY TRUCK

NOT TO BE REFERRING TO
THAT CERTAIN CLASS
OF CRITTERS

BEYOND OUR EXPECTATIONS
THINNING THE BLOOD
FOR GOOD HEALTH

HERE IS A LOVELY MORNING
BREAKFASTING WITH
GREEN TEA LEAVES

1/21/11

DESIRE THAT FEEDS THE MONSTER
ATTRACTS ALL KINDS
OF RUBBISH

GO AHEAD TAKE ADVANTAGE
OUR ANGELS WILL
HELP YOU OUT

TO LOVE WHAT YOU OWN IS TO
BEGIN TO HAVE
ALL GOOD THINGS

MAKES ENEMIES OF HIS FRIENDS
AND BEFRIENDS HIS
ENEMIES

WHOMEVER YOU LOVE IS FILLED
WITH YOUR FEELINGS
NOTHING LESS

TO EAT WHAT YOU'VE BURNED IS TO
BECOME TASTELESS
AND WASTEFUL

YOU HAVE BEEN SELECTED AS
THE CHOSEN TO
BUY BUY BUY

WHAT DELIGHT ARE WE SHARING
TO OWN THIS DAY
DEAREST ONE ?

WE'VE GOT TO GET SOME SOUL IN
OUR LIFE AND LIFE
IN OUR SOUL

YOU DON'T WANT TO MESS WITH THEM
THEY ARE SACRED
FOREVER

SHE IS GOING TO BE A
FREE BEE CHANTING
SACRED SONGS

WERE WE TO BE GROWN AS FOOD
FROM THE VERY
BEGINNING ?

THANK YOU FOR CALLING WE'LL ALL
CELEBRATE THIS
VICTORY

TO GET CAUGHT UP IN THE LOOP
LOCATE EARTHBOUND
ENTITIES

HE LIKES TO THINK CRYSTALS ARE
IMPLANTED IN
HIS FOREHEAD

ENTER TO EXPERIENCE
YOUR DWELLING FOR
O B E

1/22/11

THE HARMONIC OM WAH ONG
OPENS UP THE
CROWN CHAKRA

LOOK AT THAT MOUTH IT CAN HOLD
NINETY PERCENT
OF HIS BRAIN

YOU'VE GOT TO BE SPECIAL TO
BE HANDLING THE
REAL GOOD STUFF

WE'VE COME DOWN HERE FOR A GOOD
VACATION BUT
NOT THAT LOOK

SOFT REALITY ENTERS
INTO IT WHEN
BABY SHOWS

WHEN THEY COOK ENOUGH TO EAT
IT'S THE BEAST THAT'S
SATISFIED

TOO CONTRAINDICATIVE
A CROSS WORD PUZZLE
SCREWED THIS

TAKEN OFF FOR MEXICO
LIKE A COUPLE
OF SNOW BIRDS

1/23/11

THESE ARE REALLY SHARP PEOPLE
THEY KNOW HOW TO
DISSEMBLE

WE DON'T PLAY FAVORITES HERE
WE PLAY WHAT THEY
WANT TO HEAR

ISN'T THAT FUNNY SHE TELLS
HIM WHAT HE WANTS
HER TO THINK

THEY THINK THAT HE'S AWAKENED
BUDDHA'S NOT ALL
THAT BAD NOW

HE MUST HAVE JOINED EVERY
CULT SINCE HIS OWN
INCEPTION

THE ONLY THINGS THAT CAUSE FEAR
ARE THOSE WE THINK
WE MIGHT OWN

DO YOU REALLY HAVE TO LOVE
THEM BECAUSE THEY
NEED SO MUCH ?

DWELLING CLOSE TO SACRED SIGHTS
HELPS TO MAKE UP
MYSTERIES

REALLY IMPRESSIVE DOES IT
EVER OCCUR
ON THIS EARTH ?

REVOLUTION'S HAVE SIMPLE
AFFIRMATIONS
REVOLVING

OF COURSE THEY GET PAID SOMETHING
FOR SPENDING ALL
THAT MOOLAH

THE BEST APPROACH TO LIFE IS
THE DIGITAL
RECORDING

MAINTAINING THE ILLUSION
FOR FEAR OF CHANGE
SNOT LUFFELY

WHILE LACKING IDENTITY
WERE NO LIGHTING
MALFUNCTIONS

HE KNOWS WHAT HE'S DOING SO
NO ONE ELSE CAN
FIGURE HIM

THIS POWERFUL REMINDER
MEANS THAT THEIR CULT
IS KAPUT

THE MISINFORMATION AGE
WILL BE SAVING
LITTLE ELSE

IT WAS IN HERO WORSHIP
HE MADE IT AS
THE PARENT

PLAYING ORGELING ORTZELS
WITH WHOMEVER
WON'T BITE YOU

MUCH IN LIFE IS PERSONAL
OBSERVATION
AT ITS BEST

BIG ROUND MEN ARE ATTEMPTING
TO MAKE THEMSELVES
SEEM PREGNANT

SUCH INTERESTING DOGMAS
LEGALESE AND
PEKINESE

1/24/11

WHAT IS YOUR HIGHEST PURPOSE
DEVA'S FUSION
ABSORPTION ?

IT'S NEVER TOO HARD TO TRY
SMILE AT YOUR OWN
MISFORTUNE

WHAT THEY EXPECT TO BECOME
IS SOMEONE WHOM
THEY ARE NOT

OUR HEAVY LAUGHS AT TROUBLES
IN ORDER TO
DISPELL THEM

HE LOOKED UNDER THE EX WORDS
TO FIND TWITTY'S
BRILLIANT NAME

THEY SAY HE'S AN ECCENTRIC
FOUND HIS LONG LIST
OF DEAD ZONES

STOP RUNNING WAY OUT THERE
YOU HAVE ONLY
HERE TO GO

SONGSTERS HAVE THEIR CRITIQUES PERKED
IT'S BRAZEN THOUGH
SAGACIOUS

FAR FROM BEING DISCRETE HIS
SHOT ACROSS HER
BOW BLEW IT

THE FEMALE WHO PREFERS HER
MEN ELITE WON'T
PUT THEM DOWN

TO WHAT OBLIGATORY
LOVE DO WE OWE
THIS PLEASURE ?

CHOOSING HOW TO SELL THEIR JUNK
ACCOMPLISHING
SHEAR PINACHE

THE ORIGINAL MAY BE
UGLY BUT IT
CONTAINS PROOF

MOVING ON IS AN INTER
DIMENSIONAL
KIND OF THING

THEY TRY TO KIDNAP OUR GOATS
THEN WE BURN TIRES
IN THE ROAD

GOVERNMENT INSTALLS MARTIAL
LAW TO BAN HOT
CHOCOLATE

AVERAGE SELF PITY'S NOT
AMERICANS'
BRAND OF ANGST

DO YOU THINK THERE'S A PROBLEM ?
DON'T WORRY YOU'LL
LOCATE ONE

1/25/11

THEY'RE SPIRITUALLY BETTER OFF
KNOWING THEY CAN'T
HAVE IT ALL

WE'VE BROUGHT HIM BACK NOW THE MUSE
RESURRECTS THE
LYRIC REALM

HAVE YOU DECIDED TO HAVE
PERFECTION WHERE
THERE WAS CRUD ?

BIG WORD THAT ELITISM
LESS SELECTIVE
THAN PIGHEAD

HE PREFERS ENLIGHTENMENT
NON OVERTLY
MANIFEST

ONE OF THEIR PURPOSES HERE
EXACERBATES
OUR PROBLEM

SCREAMS MIGHT BE REFERRING TO
PARTICULAR
CHARACTERS

WE DO WANT TO BOND WITH LOVE
HAPPY TO LIVE
WITH YOU ALL

EVEN THOUGH HE DID NOT WRITE
ANY OF THESE
HE RECITES

THIS COLLECTION IS TO BE
DEDICATED
TO SHNOOKUMS

HE WILL NOT BE RETURNING
THIS LIFE TRULY
OPENED HIM

WHAT ORTZEL FIRST AGREES TO
SHE ALWAYS DOES
DIFFERENTLY

SINCE WE WON'T CAPITULATE
CAN'T THEY SIMPLY
ACQUIESCE ?

NOT SAYING IT'S YOUR FAULT BUT
WE LOST IT 'CAUSE
YOU BLEW IT

QUESTION THE COST EFFECTIVE
NATURE OF THEIR
BUG SHELTER

FUNNY HOW OUR LIVES BECOME
TWISTED AROUND
WITH THIS SCHEME

1/26/11

HAVE NO FEAR ANIMALS COME
HERE TO KEEP YOU
COMPANY

WE KNOW WHAT YOU ARE DOING
PLEASE EXPLAIN THIS
TO OUR FRIENDS

THEY'LL FIND THE SECRET TO THE
UNIVERSE IT'S
ENCODED

IT'S AS IF THEY BEAT AROUND THE
THE BUSH WITHOUT
A GAME PLAN

PLAY THAT SONG IN A AND D
TO JUMP START YOUR
D N A

IT SEEMS LIKE ALL THOSE ERRORS
NEVER OCCURRED
THEY'VE MESSED UP

HIS EARS WON'T GRAVITATE TOWARDS
PRECONCEPTUAL
TYPE NOTIONS

THERE ARE THREE DIFFERENT SONGS FOR
THIS MELODY
SO COMPOSED

NOTHING EVER HAPPENS HERE
UNLESS IT'S FOR
A GOOD TIME

OLD BOYS CAN'T WRITE A SINGLE
SONG WITHOUT A
BEER IN THERE

CATS WILL RETURN TO THE NIGHT
THAT SHINES FROM UP
ABOVE US

GROWING HIS BEARD APPEARED AS
VAINGLORIOUS
A HIDEOUT

IS THAT YOUR SUBTLETY OR
BOLD INFLECTION
OF GENRE ?

THEY'RE ROLLING IN THE SPIRIT
OF SOULS PLUCKED FROM
THEIR MOORINGS

SNOW IS WARMER THAN THE COLD
RATHER HAVE IT
SNOW THAN COLD

THOSE PREORDAINED SENTIMENTS
CONTROLLING THEM
POSED PROBLEMS

1/27/11

YOU KNOW WHAT THEY'RE UP TO BUT
TRY MAKING SOME
SENSE FOR THEM

WE MIGHT NOT UNDERSTAND BUT
THIS IS COMING
FROM BIRD BRAINS

THERE ARE ALL KINDS OF ORTZELS
SOME LIKE TO BE
SONOROUS

PREFERS GIN AND TONIC BUT
IF ALL YOU HAVE
IS HUMOR

YOU WANT A SPIRITUAL PATH
YOU'D BETTER BE
ON YOUR WAY

BUBBA'S GOT A WAYS TO GO
DETOURS CREATE
ALL THE FUN

PARANOID CONSIRACY
FOLKS ARE NOT THEIR
CUP OF CHAI

REVERED MAHAYANA KNOWS
HINAYANA'S
LITTLE QUIRKS

HE'S SUBJECT TO BE RIPPED OFF
BUT ONLY ON
HIS OWN TERMS

IF YOU BOTHER TO ASK THEM
THEY CAN REVEAL
YOUR GAME PLAN

SMILE UPON ENTERING THE
UNIFIED FIELD'S
CONSCIOUSNESS

HUBRIS DOES NOT CARRY US
BEYOND CONCERNS
OF THE BOD

GAIN FORGIVENESS AND RELEASE
IT'S CATCHING THE
HEAVY FISH

1/28/11

ETERNAL LAW COMMANDS US
BECOME THAT WHICH
DISSOLVES GUILT

TO SOLVE LOOPS WORKING THROUGH
THESE HOOKS REQUIRES
SOMETHING MORE

GROUPS APPEAR ENTICING AND
ALTOGETHER
DEVIOUS

CONDITIONS OF PURE JOY GUIDE
US ONLY TO
SALVATION

WOULDN'T IT BE NICE IF THAT
DEVICELESS FRIEND
WERE HERE NOW

THE DOG BEGINS TO LICK YOU
IT IS THEIR PLOY
TO FEED THEM

COME ON MOSES GET ROLLING
THERE'S MILES TO GO
'FORE DINNER

THERE'S NEVER BEEN A RAVING
IDENTITY
CRISIS HERE

WE MIGHT WANT TO EXPRESS OUR
HIGHEST PURPOSE
WITH INTENT

IT'S GREAT FOR KEEPING YOUR MIND
FROM WHAT YOU SHOULD
BE DOING

YOU CAN DO WHATEVER YOU
WANT TO THAT'S THE
AWE FILLED TRUTH

WHEN THEY SAY THEY UNDERSTAND
IT MEANS THEY THINK
YOU'RE BONKERS

WE'VE NOT DISAPPOINTED BY
THIS AMAZING
CONDITION

THAT IS CHARMING JUST LIKE HER
CLEOPATRA
STYLE COMPLEX

FIRST AMERICAN CULTURE
TO HAVE THEIR OWN
STATE OF ART

BLEW THEIR EARS OUT WITH THAT SONG
THEY HAVEN'T HEARD
ANYTHING

1/29/11

DRIVING THROUGH SNOW COVERED HILLS
SEARCHING THE CLIFFS
FOR BLUE ICE

MIGHT THEY MAKE OVER THAT OLD
PAMPERED BREED OF
SOCIAL DEAL ?

CONTESTANTS HAVE NOW ARRIVED
AND ATTEND THE
ORTZEL BEE

HE MUST HAVE BEEN THAT BAD BOY
USHERING IN
THE NEW AGE

AT LAST THE KIDS ARE GONE FROM
HOME AND ARE OUT
IN THEIR OWN

FINAL SOLUTIONS SURFACE
WITH THE CULTURE'S
UNDOING

SHE COULD NEVER BE HERSELF
KNOWING HOW SHE
FEELS LIKE THEM

THEY CAME TO IDOLIZE HIM
JEALOUS OF HIS
HOLINESS

HIS DREAMING SEEMED INCOMPLETE
RETURNING HIM
TO SLUMBER

AGING PERFORMER LOST AT
SEA IN STORM OF
SYMPATHY

DON'T CATCH POLAR BEAR DISEASE
FOREWARNED ABOUT
THE ARK TIC

DIANA LOVES TO BOND WITH
MALE PREDATORS
ON THE HUNT

SOME OF THEM EXPECT FAME FOR
THEIR FAVORITE
SELFLESSNESS

DID SHE WANT TO USE HIM OR
WAS IT HER HEART'S
AMBITION ?

HEAVEN WAS THE ONLY THING
HE DIDN'T TRY
TO MESS UP

SHE PLAYS HER ROLL ON THE STAGE
PERFECT OUTCAST
OTHERWISE

Phylo Ray

1/30/11

THEIR OBSESSIVE COMPULSIVE
BEHAVIOR CAN
HELP TO WIN

HE WAS THE MOST PERFECT TEN
LACKING COURAGE
SMACKED AGAIN

SHARING SOME INTRIGUING TEXT
THEIR DESIGN FOR
PEACE ON EARTH

SHE MUST BE HANGING AROUND
THAT REGISTERED
LIVE IN BAT

IT WAS THE REAL WAILING TYPE
SIREN FROM THAT
SURREAL FILM

PEOPLE CAN BE SO FRIENDLY
IN WINTERTIME
JAMAICA

IT'S EASY ASSUMING THAT
YOU CAN TRAIN THE
MAN EATER

1/31/11

DOES LIGHTING INCENSE BRING BACK
YOUR MENTOR WHO
HAD ESCAPED ?

BIRD TRIBES BECOME HAPPIER
EVERY DAY IT
LIGHTENS UP

CRASHING BANK GO BAD WHEN THE
MONEY MAN HE
GO WAY SAD

DAVIE POODGIE PAH ENJOYS
LITTLE DICKENS
BABY BURPS

ENJOYED THOSE INTUITIVE
CRAZY DUDES WHO
DONE DUDE IT

CAME ACROSS THEIR PALEO
COLLATERAL
IMPRESSIONS

CAN'T HELP WATCHING SOMEONE WHO
IS VIGILANT
GETTING BORED

NEVER THOUGHT ABOUT NATURE
CERTAINLY'S GOT
SOME EGO

WE DON'T NEED THEIR GUARANTEES
CAN DANCE OUR WAY
OUT OF HERE

D'YOU THINK HUMANS HAVE REAL VIEWS
LOOK AROUND SEE
WHAT YOU GET ?

SOME THOUGHTS THAT COME OUT THE WRONG
WAY YOU KNOW THEY
KIND OF STINK

IT MUST BE REAL GOOD CHEW SINCE
IT KEEPS OUR MINDS
ON THIS TRACK

2/01/11

THESE WORK EVEN WHEN THERE ARE
HYSTERICAL
REACTIONS

LIFE IS NOW YOUR HANDMAIDEN
BE IT SO FINE
BRING HER ON

SHE KNOWS HOW TO ROW HER BOAT
GENTLY DOWN THE
RAGING BROOK

IN THE VERY BEGINNING
DUMB DE DUMB DUMB
DUMB DE DUMB

REVOLVING TO LEARN CONTRA
DICTION CAN SPIN
STARTLING TRUTHS

WE DON'T MIND OTHER PEOPLE'S
EMPOWERMENT
NOW DO WE ?

YES AFFIRMATIONS PROCLAIM
IN PERFECT FAITH
THEY POSSESS

GREAT IMAGINATION PROVES
PEOPLE CAN BE
SPIRITUAL

HOW DO INEVITABLE
TRANSITIONS GET
HANDLED HERE ?

THIS ONE MEANS TO SHOCK US WITH
REALITY
AT ITS BEST

ORTZELS TEND TO HAVE FEATHERS
GROWING MOSTLY
FROM THEIR CHESTS

DON'T MIND IF CONSPIRACY
THEORY CAUSES
HEART ATTACKS

LET US BECOME ECSTATIC
SO THAT WARS CAN'T
BE FOUGHT HERE

YOU CAN FORGET IT IF YOU
WANT TO LET GO
OF THE PAST

THIS ALTERED DIMENSION IS
TOLERABLY
DISTINCTIVE

THE TRUE MYSTERY REMAINS
BEYOND MORTAL
AWARENESS

2/02/11

WE'VE TRIED TO COMPREHEND HOW
JESUS WAS NOT
MERELY MAN

WAS IT THEIR DESIRE TO HAVE
HIM FOR LUNCH OR
SOMETHING ELSE ?

HERE COMES THE BENEFICENT
SOUL QUESTOR TO
RETRIEVE US

FEE FIE FOH FUM SOMETHING WILL
BRING YOU TO YOUR
ASCENSION

TRANSMUTING DESIRE FROM THE
DELUSIONAL
REALMS SO THERE

SUBTLE AWARENESS IN DREAMS
MEANS TO MASTER
YOUR BRAIN WAVES

EGOS THAT FEEL TROUBLED MIGHT
HAVE SOME REAL NEED
TO GET SHRUNK

WE HAVE HAD ENOUGH KARMA
SEARCHING THERE FOR
YOUR DHARMA

LOOSH IS PROVIDING EVERY
GOOD SUBSTANCE WE
ARE MADE OF

PERPETUAL CONSCIOUSNESS BLOWS
IN A WIND CALLED
NIRVANA

2/03/11

THEY DON'T WANT US TO TELL THEM
WHERE TO GO FOR
SELF ESTEEM

WHY BOTHER TO CRITIQUE IT
WHEN YOU CAN JUST
FLUSH IT DOWN ?

TO CREATIVE MINDS YOU ARE
A BRIDGE ACROSS
THE ABYSS

THE DISTANCE BETWEEN LOVE AND
BASIC GOODNESS
IS CRUCIAL

2/04/11

THE ORGELING ORTZELS ARE
GAINING KNOWLEDGE
OF THEIR OWN

SOME OVERT PERFECTION IS
PREVENTING AN
INTRUSION

ACHES TEND TO FEEL MUCH BETTER
PENDING FINAL
SOLUTIONS

HUMANS BECOME POWERFUL
DEMONSTRATING
FORGIVENESS

DOES THE VEHICLE MATTER
WHEN YOU KNOW HOW
TO GET THERE ?

WHAT ARE THEY GOING TO DO
AND WHO ARE THEY
DOING NOW ?

IT'S THE ELIXIR OF LIFE
WHERE IN LIES MOST
REVERIE

GO RIGHT AHEAD AND ZORCH BEER
YOU'RE CERTAINLY
DESERVING

ORTZEL MEISTERS DON'T HAVE TO
ENVISION WHO
TO BECOME

IT IS THE POTTER WHO KNOWS
THE POT WITHIN
ITS CONTENT

HER SYMPATHY CAME AROUND
TO INDULGE IN
SELF PITY

HE HAS A PLOY IT'S A LIE
AN ENTRAPMENT
KIND OF GUY

NOT TO BE IRREVERENT
NOR RACIST NOR
SEXIST BENT

BUDDHA LOVES US THIS WE KNOW
HIS BODY IS
SPIRIT THOUGH

2/05/11

INDIVIDUAL GUILT BECOMES
SEQUESTERED IN
THE JURY

THEIR BUSINESS WAS MARKETING
ROYALTY THROUGH
NOBLE TEAS

IF THIS DOES NOT THEN NOTHING
CAN TAKE OUR MINDS
FROM THIS WORLD

EVERY ROLE IS PHONY
HOW DO WE ALL
GET TO PLAY ?

ORTZELS GO 'ROUND AND AROUND
READY TO AIM
FIRE AT WILL

THE ONLY THING FRESH ABOUT
THESE VEGGIES IS
ATTITUDE

RUNAWAY MINDS CONNECT TO
TECHNOCRATS WITH
COME ALONGS

IT WAS THAT HIMALAYAN
SAGE WHO APPEARS
YETI LIKE

BEARS ARE REAL TOP CRITTERS FOR
SHAPESHIFTERS TO
PRACTICE WITH

PERSONAS FREQUENTLY MAKE
CORRELATIONS
WITH WALKINS

SHE'S ABOUT TO FIND HERSELF
BEING RAPTURED
NONE THE LESS

HE KNOWS WHERE HE IS GOING
MIND AND BODY
CONTEMPLATE

2/06/11

ARE THERE NO NON ENTITIES
POWERS THAT BE
PLEASE ANSWER ?

YOUR FOLLOWING CAN SWIM IN
THE STREAM OF THEIR
CONCIOUSNESS

HIGHLY SUSPECT OF BEING
DEEMED CLASSIC YET
CLASSICAL

BEWARE WIZARDS AND WITCHES
THE TITANS ARE
OUT TO PLAY

THE MEANS FOR RESEARCHING JOY
ACCOMPLISHES
COMPLEXES

REINVENTING LANGUAGE WITH
COLLOQUIAL
COMPLIANCE

WE HAVE NOT REACHED A ZILLION
SO MUCH FOR OUR
NATION'S DEBT

FREEDOM OF THOUGHT REVEALS OUR
MORE SENSITIVE
SOGGY HEARTS

HOLD ONTO SOMEONE WHEN YOU
START TO LAUGH LIKE
THAT SILLY

THERE'S LITTLE DIFFICULTY
WITH CONFUSING
SOLITUDES

JOCULAR BEAST BRINGS HUMOR
TO A POINT OF
THE UNKNOWN

HAVE TO GO STRAIGHT FOR A TIME
PERHAPS A MILE
OR MORE SO

HE REALIZED THAT HIS NIGHTMARE
COULD BE TRAINED BY
WHISPERING

GOD GRANTS YOUR BLESSING SO THAT
CONFUSION WILL
CLARIFY

IF WE HOPE TO FIND THE WAY
THEN WE MUST GIVE
UP SOMEONE

THEY HAVE NOTHINGNESS TO SHOW
AND CERTAINLY
CAN NOT TELL

2/07/11

EXPECTATION EXPLORES OUR
HIATUS FOR
THE MIDPOINT

RHYMES DON'T MEAN TOO MUCH AND TEND
TO FORM LITTLE
MORE THAN EASE

POLITICOS FILLED WITH PRIDE
SUPPORT SOME TRITE
RENDITIONS

WE HAVE OUR FIELD OF FLOWERS
THANKS TO MOTHER
NATURE'S SEED

PROVOKED SOLICITATION
DRIVES THE HERD THROUGH
TEMPTATION

SHE'LL BE GREAT AT TEACHING SAX
EDUCATION
WITH THAT JAZZ

YOU HAVE OBTAINED A VIEW THAT
APPEARS TO BE
QUITE VACANT

YOUR SEARCH FOR TRUTH BEHIND THE
IDEA CAN
RAMBLE ON

2/08/11

DREAMLESS WAS SUFFERING FROM
SUBCONSCIOUS MOOD
SUPPRESSION

SLIM JIM MANAGED TO SLIP THROUGH
EVERY CRACK OF
THAT WEIRDNESS

HE TRIED TO APOLOGIZE
FROM THE REAR END
OF THE DOG

WE DON'T RECOGNIZE THEM AS
HUMAN BUT THEY
CAN SMELL US

EVERYTHING IS BIPOLAR
WHETHER WE LIKE
THEM OR NOT

LIFE TIME UPON LIFE TIME MEANS
THE WHOLE THING HAS
ROTTED OUT

ALL THAT'S LEFT TO DO IS TO
LOOSEN IT UP
WITH YOUR MIND

WHEN IS HE GOING TO WEAR
HIS BELT AND STOP
MOONING US ?

THEY'LL PUT THIS TOWN ON THE MAP
BY PROVIDING
BIG DISCOUNTS

IF THESE SEEDS DECIDE TO SPROUT
YOU'LL WANT TO TAKE
A LOOK SEE

IT'S THAT ONE SIDED KIND OF
CONVERSATION
DON'T YOU KNOW

THAT RESTAURANT PRICES MEALS
ACCORDING TO
CALORIES

ARE YOU SURE WE'RE LIVING CLOSE
ENOUGH ON THE
BORDERLINE ?

LIVE FOR EXCLUSIVITY
DON'T PLAN TO BE
SATISFIED

IT MUST BE NICE SEDUCED BY
ALL THIS STUFF IT''S
WHY WE'RE HERE

PEOPLE REFLECTING THAT YOU
WERE WRONG NOT TO
THINK THEM RIGHT

THEY WANT YOU TO BECOME THE
BODISATVA
THAT IS ALL

EVERYTIME WE MEET SHAKTI
YOU THINKS SHE'S STONED
AMNESTY ?

2/09/11

EMPIRES ARE MAINTAINED THROUGH THE
RULERS' CAREFUL
THUGGERY

EVERYONE WHO HAS LIVED ON
THE EARTH IS HERE
AT THIS TIME

WHOM EVER BELIEVES IN LOVE
WILL BE WITH GOD
CHUGGING THIS

THERE MIGHT BE A RAINBOW TO
FIND WHEN THE STORM
BLOWS OVER

IT CAN BE MORE THAN FUN TO
MANUFACTURE
YOUR HEAVEN

PREPARING SOUTHERN SPICE RUB
HEATS A WHOLE LOT
OF YER MEAT

WE APPARENTLY HAVE OUR
GRAND DHARMA TO
CONSIDER

ABUSE CAME OUT JUSTIFIED
BUT WHO BITES THE
BULLET NOW ?

WHAT ARE WE DOING ROAMING
THROUGH LIFETIMES TO
RE ACCESS ?

HE GIVES HER DIVINE STATUS
SHE OFFERS HIM
PROTECTION

2/10/11

GO AHEAD AND GENERATE
SHARE WITH THOSE WHO
CHOOSE TO LOVE

HI THERE THIS IS YOUR SNOW WHITE
ARE YOU SLEEPY
OR DOPY ?

FALLING FOR CUTE APPRAISALS
ONLY PERCEIVES
DEFICITS

HAVING RESTED THEIR BELLIES
ON SOMETHING THEY'VE
CROSSED THEIR ARMS

THAT SHARP CONSTITUENCY
IS BOUND TO WORK
ITS WAY OUT

2/11/11

WITH THAT CONFABULATION
THEIR FAITH IS REAL
RELIGIOUS

THOSE WEREN'T MEANT JUST TO SHOCK US
REALITY
AT ITS BEST

LEADERS POSSESSED BY EGO
PROVE TO BE MOST
HAZARDOUS

NO PROBLEM CATCHING THE OLD
SOUTHERN COMFORT
MIASMA

THOUGH HE LOVED THEM MOST DEARLY
THEY LIBELED HIM
WITH NO SOUL

MOTHER DESIRED HER DAUGHTER
TO BECOME MORE
THAN A MAN

ASKING WHERE TO FIND IT THEY
DID NOT WANT TO
BE SITED

DON'T RECOGNIZE THERAPY
BUT ENJOY IT
THOROUGHLY

THAT FORTUNE COOKIE WARNED TO
LEAVE BEHIND YOUR
FANTASIES

MAY BE THEY DON'T UNDERSTAND
POLLY WANNA
BIG CRACKER

THE MOST BEAUTIFUL BEINGS
WILL NEVER SAY
ALL THAT MUCH

SEARCHING FOR LITERARY
GENIUS RATHER
THAN PROWESS

CRYING OUT LOUD POETRY'S
DIALECTIC
DIARY

2/12/11

IT'S A MINUS TEN IN TOWN
NORTHEAST KINGDOM'S
COZY NEST

HE'S NOT DONE WITH THE SCHMALTZ YET
LET THEM CAN THE
SARCASM

THE COURT TENDS TO RECOGNIZE
PRIMA FACIE
BRAIN DAMAGE

TALKS LIKE THAT IN ORDER TO
ATTRACT PROPER
CUSTOMERS

PROPOSALS TO LORD RAMA
FOUNDED THIS HERE
UNIVERSE

RELIGIOUS GOINGS ON ARE
NOW TO BE HELD
IN HEAVEN

THE GURU WILL PROTECT US
INSIDE A PEARL
OF BLUE LIGHT

THE ONE WHO LAUGHS THE LOUDEST
ENDS UP RUNNING
THEIR WHOLE SHOW

THERE WILL ALWAYS BE MORE JAMS
FUNKY CRITTERS
AND WHAT NOT

SHAKE HANDS AND COME OUT FIGHTING
YOU MIGHT ALSO
WANT TO FLOAT

THEY MUST FIGURE SOME LICENSE
CERTIFIES THEIR
HOLINESS

CHUMP'S ENTIRELY CAPABLE
MEDIATING
YOUR BREAKUP

THE EASIEST PLACE TO LIVE
IS WHERE NO ONE
WANTS TO GO

PIGHEAD PRACTICED THOSE CURES AND
CALAMITY
RELENTED

IT'S ALWAYS FOR THE BETTER
SEEMS ONE WAY OR
THE OTHER

WAIT FOR YOUR SCIENCE FICTION
TO TURN INTO
A LIFESTYLE

THEY DON'T WISH TO TRAIN WITH HIM
HE'S SUCH A NON
ALIEN

NO HEART BLEEDS MORE PROFUSELY
THAN THE ONE BLEEDS
FOR ITSELF

SO WHAT'S WRONG WITH THOSE EXPERTS
THEY'RE NUTS JUST LIKE
ALL THE REST

LIFE'S NOT SUPPOSED TO MAKE SENSE
BUT DON'T WORRY
IT WILL PASS

IT'S ANIMAL POISE THAT THOSE
DANCING GIRLS ARE
PERFORMING

IF WE CAN'T BEGIN TO LOVE
OUR SAVIOUR WILL
LEAVE US HERE

SURVIVING ON THE EDGE WHERE
THERE'S SUFFICIENT
SUBSISTENCE

OUR MANDALA WILL ASCEND
WITH PERPETUAL
CONSCIOUSNESS

MORE OBDURATE THAN GRANITE
LOVE CAN ENDURE
LOTS OF ROCKS

PEARLS DON'T GROW ON THE SURFACE
SOME ONE HAS TO
DIVE FOR THEM

RETURNING BEYOND LIFE TIMES
PRUDENTIALLY
YOU ARE THERE

SO MUCH LOVE HAS SEEPED IN HERE
CAN WE CLEAN UP
YOUR ACT NOW ?

THE INCINERATOR CAN'T
BE STOPPED TO FIND
YOUR FLASH DRIVE

HE WOULD OPEN UP A VEIN
FOR A FRIEND OR
ANYONE

THIS DISH IS SO POWERFUL
REMINDS US OF
GREAT CUISINE

NARCISSUS INDIE SINGER'S
LOUD VOICE IMPLIES
NOT SO GREAT

SHE WOULD RATHER MOVE THAN TO
LIVE WITH HER SICK
PERSONA

WHAT HE CAN DO IS SPECIAL
HE KNOWS THAT AS
HE MUMBLES

CONGRATULATE HER WHEN YOU
FIND ORTZEL AND
KEEP IT CLOSE

SAFE ENOUGH TO SAY MIGHT BE
SUFFERING FROM
CONUNDRUMS

THE ONES WHO ARE NATURAL
ICONOCLASTS
PLEASE BLESS THEM

HE MADE THEM BELIEVE THAT HE
WAS SOMEBODY
ALL TOGETHER

THERE'S ALWAYS BEEN A TREATISE
ON ENTERING
THEIR HEAVEN

CULTIVATING CONSCIOUSNESS
REQUIRES WEEDING
COME TO THINK

HERE'S TO MISUNDERSTANDING
INNUMERABLE
VICTORIES

HE SAID DO YOUR OWN THING MAN
WITH GENUINE
CONTENTMENT

2/13/11

WHEN WE ARE LOVING SOMEONE
IT CAN HELP TO
SOLVE PROBLEMS

2/14/11

LEARNING TO LOVE POSSESSIONS
TAKE YOUR TIME WITH
THE CLEARINGS

2/15/11

DANCED PROVERBIAL CIRCLES
AROUND YOUR VAIN
NEOPHYTE

THEY ARE MEDITATORS AND
SOMETIMES THEY DO
RELIGION

WHATEVER HAPPENS DON'T FEEL
BAD WHEN THEY CAN'T
STAND YOUR VOICE

WHO KNEW THE WORLD WOULD CONSPIRE
TO CONDEMN ITS
RESIDENTS

THESE ARE HARD LESSONS TO LEARN
SO CARRY THEM
TENDERLY

LIVING IN THE LOVELIEST
PLACE LABELLED YOUR
INNER MOST

NO FAULT FOUND WITH BUDDHISM
ALL AMOUNTS TO
EMPTINESS

IS IT THE THIEF IN THE NIGHT
HAS THE COURAGE
TO STEAL LIGHT ?

THEY SIMPLY DON'T UNDERSTAND
NOT ENTIRELY
EXPECTED

2/16/11

COULD NOT SIMPLY BE SEDUCED
BUT HAPPENED TO
FALL INTO

FIND YOURSELF IN THEIR WORLDLY
STRONGHOLD THAT YOU
MIGHT ESCAPE

WE WANT TO THANK YOUR BUSINESS
FOR HELPING US
TO TAKE OFF

THE BEST WAY TO BE IS TO
SMILE IN THE FACE
OF YOUR SAINT

PROCRASTINATION THAT IS
TO REPROACH WITH
DECENCY

WHEN YOU DO WHAT THEY EXPECT
YOU CAN CALL THEM
ANY TIME

SINCE WHEN DID THEIR LAH LAH LAND
APPEAR NOT TO
HAVE RETURNED ?

HERE'S ONE OF THE MOST BRILLIANT
WINDMILL SLAYERS
OF ALL TIME

SHE'S A RIOT OF A COOK
KILLING YOU WITH
HER MENU

INCOMPARABLE BURPS CAN BE
COMBINED WITH THE
BABA SOUND

NOPE WE'RE NOT TOO EARLY BUT
PERHAPS IT'S A
BIT TOO LATE

FEW MANIPULATIONS HAVE
OBSESSED TO MESS
UP THEIR MIND

FATHER'S GONE OVER THE TOP
FACILITATE
YOUR END GAME

2/17/11

GIVEN TOO MUCH FREEDOM THEY
HAVE REVELLED THEN
WENT MISSING

2/18/11

BHAKTI YOGA'S SACRED SOUND
AWAKENS THE
INNER CHILD

THEY WERE WAITING IN THE BUS
STATION WHEN THEIR
SHIP CAME IN

GOING WHERE OUTDOOR SHOES ARE
ALL THE SHOES ARE
OUTDOORS' NOW

PRETTY LITTLE GIRL WITH A
PRESSURE COOKER
KIND OF MIND

ONE ADVANTAGE CAN BE DEEMED
MORE FAVORABLE
THAN OTHERS

LAUGHING YOGA EXERCISE
IS OLD LIKE THE
VERY HILLS

2/19/11

SHE WAS IN HER BODY BUT
GAVE IT UP FOR
ASCENSION

WE SUPPOSE THIS IS ABOUT
YOUR BELOVED'S
TRUE MONSTER

IN SOME INSTANCES HE'S STRANGE
ILLUMINED IN
THOSE OTHERS

WE'RE SORRY THAT YOU ARE GOD
CAN WE HELP YOU
OUT OF IT ?

THEY'RE NOT WALKING THEIR TALK 'CAUSE
THEY'RE NOT EVEN
TALKING NOW

STRANGELY STUFFED COMMENTARY
OPEN ENDED
MOCKERY

THEIR ONLY OBLIGATION
TO STRAIGHTEN UP
WHILE LAUGHING

YOU'RE RIGHT ABOUT PREDATORS
IT'S THE NATURE
OF THE BEAST

FILLED WITH IMAGINATION
LITTLE FOOL AND
DIAPERS FULL

HE HAD NO DESIRE TO CATCH
IDENTITY
IN CRISIS

IMAGINE BEING BORN ON
THE TOUR AT A
TIME LIKE THIS

SINGING TWIRLING AND DANCING
WITH POWER IN
HER EIGHT ARMS

YOUR INTERPRETATION OF
THE WORD SOUNDS TOO
ICONIC

BELOVED HELPING SPIRITS
WHO WILL YOU SAVE
THIS FINE DAY ?

POISED TO STRIKE ABOVE THE HEAD
IRONICAL
DAMOCLES

YOU CAN'T DIE IF YOU'RE OUT OF
YOUR BODY A
NO BRAINER

WHEN SHE GOT PREGNANT HE KEPT
PILING IT ON
TO KEEP PACE

WHAT DOES THAT AMORPHOUS KIND
OF LOVE LIKE TO
INDULGE IN ?

HE PLAYS ACCOMPANYMENT
PIANO TO
DOG'S HOWLING

SOME OF THESE ARE MUCH BETTER
ORGELING WITH
THAN OTHERS

HIS OUTRAGEOUS NERVE SOMEHOW
FLIPPED HIM ON HIS
CANOGGIN

TURNS OUT WE DON'T NEED EGO
TO GIVE UP ALL
THE FEAR BASE

SOMETHING IN US DOES NOT CHANGE
ALL IT DOES IS
TO RECALL

DOES HE WANT EVERYONE TO
FALL FOR HIM WE'LL
ALL GO DOWN ?

IS THE RIGHT WAY TO PROCEED
MORE LIKE SOMEONE
ELSE'S GUESS ?

2/20/11

WALKING THE PATH TOGETHER
COMING UPON
SOLID ICE

NOTHING BUT FROZEN HEARTS THERE
TRY TO APPLY
SOME FRICTION

ALL THAT WE CAN DO IS WAIT
AND LINGER OUT
IN THE STORM

KNOCK OURSELVES OUT WITH THE STUFF
THAT TRULY
TURNS YOU ON

WE CAN ALL GET TOGETHER
IN REMEMBRANCE
ACCEPTANCE

TRY OUT THE HIGHER DESIGN
MIGHT SERVE YOU WELL
IN THE END

DOES THE PETITE BOURGEOISIE
QUALIFY THEIR
OLYMPICS ?

NANNIES HAVE BEEN TRAINED TO HUNT
INCOMPETENT
NANOTECHS

CHARM WAS THE TRUTH IN HER LIFE
ACTIVATING
THAT KIND CURSE

IF YOU'RE BEHIND THE MOON YOU
SERIOUSLY
WATCH YOUR BACK

IN ITS TRUE CONSEQUENCE LOVE
OBTAINS THE SOUL'S
OM MISSION

PERHAPS A BARREN SOUL MUST
TRIGGER MINDS TO
SEEK WISDOM

IT REQUIRES ONE LADLE FULL
TO RESTORE LIFE'S
DIGNITY

IF SHE WERE ME SHE WOULD MOST
LIKELY FOLLOW
WISE WOMAN

TO FIND THAT WE ARE MORTALS
CAUSES HUMAN
DILEMMA

PERCEIVE SPIRITUAL TRUTHS TO
EXPERIENCE
LIFE'S WONDERS

IF WE CHOOSE TO RUN AWAY
OUR HERITAGE
BECOMES LOST

LET THEM FEEL SO EXHALTED
TODAY AND CRY
TOMORROW

BETTER TO RECOGNIZE ALL
SENTIENT BEINGS
IN THESE THINGS

MAYBE IN THE ROCKIES WE
CAN FIND SOME KIND
OF SMART ROCKS

SHARING US MEANS THAT WE CAN
ETERNALIZE
TOGETHER

WHEN ART IS JUST A FART THEN
THE WHOLE LOT SEEMS
MUCH TOO RIPE

WHEN FORTUNE CONTAINS STRIVING
THE REST MAINTAINS
LITTLE ELSE

DEATH CEASES TO EXIST IN
THAT MODE OF STARK
SURVIVAL

WAS IT WILLIAM SHAKESPEARE'S OR
PERHAPS EDWARD
DE VERE'S SPEAR ?

FAR BETTER TO GUSH FORTH FACT
THAN TO OVER
EXTEND TRUTHS

EVERYONE IS OUR VERY
BEST THERAPIST
LEAVE IT THERE

SHE BELIEVES WINNER TAKES ALL
THEN THE BIG FISH
EATS THE SMALL

SHE'S NOT HIS MOMMY BUT HIS
DUALISTIC
CONCEPTION

YOUR LIFE BECOMES A MANTRA
EXPERIENCE
TAKES YOU THERE

WHAT BOTHERS THEM AT TIMES IS
THEY HAVE FOUND NO
GREAT DESIRE

ENTITY NON ENTITY
HOWEVER WE
PREFER IT

DON'T THEY BELIEVE THAT SOMEDAY
WE WILL BECOME
ENLIGHTENED ?

ONCE EXISTING BELIEFS WERE
MORE CLEARLY SO
VISIBLE

DON'T KNOW WHAT THEY ARE TALKING
ABOUT SINGING
IT'S JUST FINE

THE END OF THE TUNNEL IS
NOT FAR FROM ITS
BEGINNING

SLIPPERY SLOPES AND QUAKING
EARTH IT'S TERRA
SONORA

EARTH MOMMA FROM THE SIXTIES
NURTURING AND
DOPE HEADED

IT'S BEST TO BE FOUND AND NOT
LOST IN PRIVATE
SENTIMENT

THE COURSE IN GREEK ORACLES
IS PRESENTED
WHEN GAS FLOWS

RIBBIT PLAYED THE FROG UNTIL
HE LOST HIS LEGS
THEN HE CROAKED

2/21/11

THEY WONDER SOMETIMES WHO IS
HEALING THEM WITH
ALL THESE SAINTS

INGEST SOMETHING UNDERSTOOD
THEN ALTER STATES
OF KNOWING

HE MUST HAVE CLEARED HIS MIND OF
SOME BEFUDDLED
MONSTERFUL

THE PUNCH LINE IS TO EXPLAIN
CATACLYSM'S
PRINCIPLES

WE CAN GO ANYWHERE NOT
LIMITED BY
TIME NOR SPACE

IT BUGS THEM SOMETIMES THAT THEY
CAN'T FIND THEIR ROOT
OF DESIRE

ATTAIN FORGIVENESS TO MAKE
CONTACT WITH YOUR
BLESSED LIGHT

HOW DID SHE GET AWAY WITH
IT ASSUMING
SHE CRAZY ?

ASK YOURSELF WHO HIS FRIENDS ARE
THEN ASK HIM WHO
HE TALKS TO

ARROGANT ALIENS LOST
THIS EARTH TRYING
TO SHOW OFF

HANG ONTO THOSE CERTAIN ODD
IDEAS YOU
NEVER KNOW

THEY SUED HIS PANTS OFF BUT THEY
LET HIM KEEP HIS
UNDERWEAR

A TREE COULD NOT FALL IN THE
FOREST WITHOUT
AWARENESS

IT TAKES ONLY ONE BUTT HEAD
TO MAKE ALL THOSE
STRANGE NOISES

THEY DON'T HAVE THEM ANYWHERE
BUT YOU CAN FIND
IT SOMEWHERE

2/22/11

THREATENING TO KILL HER DEMONS
PREVENTED HER
SUICIDE

EVERYTHING YOU HAVE EVER
WANTED IS HERE
PLUS A FEW

2/23/11

HABITUALLY LOVING FRIENDS
PREOCCUPY
OUR BEST THOUGHTS

THEY DO NOT MEAN ANYTHING
UNLESS WE GIVE
THEM PURPOSE

SHE HAS ALWAYS BEEN OBSESSED
SINCE SHE WAS AN
AVID PUP

PROMISED THEM ENHANCED BODIES
BUT MORPHED INTO
WEIRD CYBORGS

SEEING WITH THE SOUL BEHIND
ACADEMIC
REDACTION

YOU WANT TO BE WALKING ON
THAT SUNNY SIDE
OF THE STREET

DON'T LET THE SHADOW CATCH US
I KNOW WE CAN
TURN IT ON

BODIES ARE CONNECTED WITH
BIO PHOTONS
IN THE FIELD

MEMORY NECESSITATES
THE NEED TO LIVE
ANY HOW

EPIGENE MECHANISMS
CREATE THE WORLD
AROUND US

NEVER TOO LATE TO BECOME
AWARE OF OUR
LACK OF GUILT

THE HEART'S INITIAL RESPONSE
BEATS THE CRAP OUT
OF THE BRAIN

HE DIED A THOUSAND DEATHS WHILE
HE WAITED FOR
MERCEDES

WITH ALL THOSE CHARMING SOUNDS GOD
HAS GOT TO BE
ENTERTAINED

2/24/11

AIN'T A RUG BENEATH THAT BRO
YOU KNOW HE'S BEEN
SLAMMED BEFORE

WE MIGHT MISS THE ILLUSION
HOLDING SHIELDS WITH
OUT COURAGE

THOSE FANTASIES WE DRUMMED UP
TO RATIONALIZE
EXISTENCE

HE'S DONE SO LITTLE NO ONE
HAS LOCATED
HIS IMPRINT

HIS GREATNESS WAS BORN UPON
ACCOMPLISHING
MINUTAE

MATERIAL ATTACHMENTS
MASQUERADES AS
TRUE NATURE

YOU WANT TO BE THE WINNER
HOLDING ON WILL
TAKE YOU THERE

ASKING FOR THE BLESSING IS
SOMETHING THAT WILL
BE GRANTED

YOU WANT TO SERVE SOMEBODY
BEYOND THIS HERE
ILLUSION

THE WISDOM OF CONFUSION
TRANSLATES INTO
NON ACTION

WHETHER WE CAN REMEMBER
OR NOT THAT DREAM
DID ITS WORK

INNOCENCE POSES WITHIN
LIFE THAT BECOMES
IMMORTAL

WHEN ARE THEY GOING TO STOP
ACTING LIKE SOME
NUT WHO IS ?

THE FORMLESS KNOW ALL ABOUT
OVERCOMING
SORTS OF THINGS

ANGELS CAN PLUCK THOSE HEART STRINGS
TO EVERY ONES'
CONTENTMENT

IMAGINE BUYING SOMEONE
A SHIRT INSTEAD
OF DINNER

THE WAY TO FIND OUR HEAVEN
IS TO SERVE THEM
'TIL THE END

IT WAS HER GRACE DEMANDED
TO BE ON THE
WINNING SIDE

WHO KNEW THAT PEACE WOULD BECOME
OUR SACRED LAND'S
DESTRUCTION ?

CREATIVITY NEVER
IDENTIFIES
WITH THE FACTS

KARMA HERE IS KIND OF SMOOTH
SO DON'T BE TOO
SERIOUS

CANNOT TAKE THEM WITH YOU BUT
CAN NEVER SAY
NO TO THEM

THAT'S NOT WHAT THEY ARE SAYING
TELLING YOU IT'S
IMPORTANT

GOD BLESS YOUR SOUL MY SISTERS
AND MY BROTHERS
GOD BLESS YOU

ALTHOUGH HE FELT QUITE SOUL LESS
HE COULD ATTAIN
SOME SOLACE

SOME PEOPLE HAVE THE KNACK FOR
SACRIFICING
LOWER SELVES

NOT SUPPOSED TO TEACH PERFECT
ENGLISH THAT WOULD
BE A SHAM

YOU KNOW WHEN YOU'RE IN THE ZONE
FUZZY FEELINGS
COME ALONG

SOMEONE FROM ANOTHER REALM
WILL DROP IN AND
PICK YOU UP

PERHAPS WE ARE IGNORING
THE ONE THING THAT
SEALS OUR LIVES

WHEN WE CHOOSE TO RETURN OUR
CONSCIENCE WILL NOW
RE EMERGE

TRANSFORMING VISIONS PERCEIVES
THE KINDEST WORLD'S
POTENTIAL

WE CREATE TO GREAT EXTENT
THIS LIFE THAT WE'VE
COME TO CHOOSE

WE DO WANT TO GET OUT THERE
INTO REGIONS
BEYOND SPACE

YOU'D WANT TO KNOW WHAT THEY KNOW
ABOUT WHAT THE
HEY YOU KNOW

LIVING ON THE EARTH'S THIN CRUST
VERY SHALLOW
LIFE STYLE HERE

MOST RELEVANT PRIMEVAL
DISCOVERY
IS LIKE FIRE

SO THE HORSE RADISH GIVES YOU
PRETTY GOOD KICK
IN THE PANTS ?

ONCE WE BEGIN TO GO THERE
COMPLETES ITSELF
DOWN THE ROAD

WE BEGIN TO LEARN TO LAUGH
RECOGNIZING
EACH OTHER

2/26/11

WE WOULD LIKE TO INTRODUCE
OUR FRIENDS FROM THE
SACRED REALM

THEY'VE EVERY RIGHT TO DO IT
THE WAY IT IS
TO BE DONE

YOU THINK IT MIGHT BE TIME TO
DISCONTINUE
OR TRANSMUTE ?

THE HEALING IS A VERY
COMPLEX QUESTION
IN THIS CASE

THERE'S A PECKING ORDER HERE
TO CREATE THE
DEMIGOD

TELL ME UM SAY HAVE WE FOUND
GARUDA OR
THE BUDDHA ?

TAKE A COURSE IN ORTZELING
FIND YOUR INNER
DING A LING

HE LET THEM BEAT ON HIM HEH
SACRILEGE OR
SACRE BLEU

2/27/11

TO HAVE NO IDENTITY
IS ADMISSION
TO FREEDOM

HOW DOES MA BOMBO BEGIN
HER EXTRACTION
RITUAL ?

I DON'T KNOW DO YOU KNOW ME
WHO HERE IS THE
DONUT GUY ?

AS FAR AS SELF KNOWLEDGE GOES
STUFFED BODY PARTS
DON'T SAY MUCH

ATTACHMENTS TO FRAGMENTED
BEINGS DOES NOT
TAKE US FAR

CAN INTIMACY GAMES TAKE
THE PLACE OF OUR
TRUE FRIENDSHIP

LIVED SPLENDIDLY SPENDING HER
BIG BUCKS ON THAT
PETTING ZOO

CAN SOMEONE WHO IS NOT SO
CONFUSED AVOID
THE CHAOS ?

THE JUG FILLED UP SO FAST THAT
IT COULD NOT HELP
DRIP A DROP

SHARING SUFFICIENT LOVE TENDS
TO GENERATE
DEVOTION

A FAT CAT FELL UPON THE
HOLY MOUSE THAT
ASCENDED

SITTING ON HIS LAURELS HE'S
PREVENTED FROM
FEELING DOOMED

ARE THEY DESPERATELY SEARCHING
FOR CONFLUENCE
AND SCAPEGOATS ?

IT'S LIKE BEING ANNOINTED
WITHOUT HAVING
BORN AGAINS

HE EATS THE PEACH THEN WISELY
PLANTS THE PIT IN
SOME RICH EARTH

ALL YOU'VE DONE THIS MORNING IS
TO STAND AND EAT
FOR INSTANCE

PERHAPS THEY FELT HE WAS THE
TORTURED SOUL WHEN
HE MET THEM

WHY SCREW IT UP WITH YOUR OWN
WHEN THERE'S PLENTY
OTHER MINDS

BE TRUE TO ONE'S SELF COMMEND
TO OTHERS WHEN
PLAUSIBLE

THIS TRANSLATION OF FAMOUS
QUOTES ENGENDERS
VALUABLES

SHE WANTED TO MAKE THAT TOWN
HER HOME TWAS BROUGHT
TO ITS KNEES

SHALL WE PART RIGHT NOW OR MIGHT
WE WAIT AWHILE
ASK YOUR FRIENDS ?

IT'S O K TO BE HALF CRAZED
ALONG WITH ALL
THE OTHERS

CRYING OUT LOUD IT'S THE NEW
MILLINIEM
HOWL IN TIME

2/28/11

ARE YOU HAVING SOME FUN NOW
THAT YOU'VE BECOME
THE SHRINK'S SHRINK ?

MAY GOD BE WITH THEM THEY'RE RIGHT
THEY'RE RIGHT THEY'RE WRONGED
THEY'RE WRONGED RIGHT ?

YOU'LL BECOME WHATEVER YOU
TAKE DON'T DO IT
JUST HAVE FUN

HEY HO THE BLOKES GOT IT GOOD
HE'D BETTER GET
GOING NOW

ARE THESE NEAR ENOUGH TO THE
RIVAL ORTZELS
SPELL IT OUT ?

WAS IT A SIMPLE CASE OF
DROID RAGE ON A
TENDER FOOT ?

HE IS UNIQUE AND WHAT HIS
MOTHER WANTS HIM
TO BECOME

WHAT WAS IT THE OFFICER
TOLD THEM TO SAY
SAVED THEIR SKIN ?

HE HAS MAPPED THE CRYSTAL MINE
NOW HIS GUIDE HAS
TO FIND HIM

NO PROBLEM SUBLIMATING
INTIMACY
IT'S A GAS

IS IT THAT WE GET ONLY
AS MUCH LUSCH AS
WE CAN LUFF ?

CHRIST LOVES DEVOTION WHEN IT
DEVOURS SO MUCH
DECEPTION

THEY WILL EITHER CHOOSE TO EAT
OR YOU CONSUME
THEM INSTEAD

MIGHT AS WELL POINT THEIR FINGERS
AT GOD AND SAY
YOU BAD BOY

EVERY ARTIST ENTERTAINS
DETACHMENT IN
SOLITUDE

THEY WERE HAPPY TO BECOME
CRAZY TO BE
HAPPY TOO

TELL ME BAY BAY WE HOW CAN
POSSIBLY BLOW
BLUE BUBBLES ?

EXPLAIN TO ME OUR PROBLEM
STAYING OUT OF
YOUR TROUBLES

3/01/11

PROBLEM IS IT'S NOT WHAT YOU
DON'T KNOW IT IS
HOW YOU THINK

LET ME KNOW IF WE CAN RUB
THESE TWO SOUL PARTS
TOGETHER

CINDERELLA LIVES DOWNSTAIRS
SNOW WHITE SLEEPS IN
THE GARRET

BABY TELLS ME THAT WE LIVE
TO RESPOND TO
BLAMELESS WORLDS

THIS CLOSE TO ENLIGHTENMENT
CAN THEY EVER
BE RELEASED ?

LOVELY TIME IN THE MORNING
FROGGY'S DAY TO
GO COURTING

3/02/11

RELAXATION CAN PUT YOU
IN A GOOD MOOD
SLOTHFUL HURTS

THEY DON'T WANT THEIR HUMAN RIGHTS
NOT VERY MUCH
HARDLY SO

TRUE STORY WHY SHOULD THEY LIE
DOES'NOT BEGIN
TO HELP THEM

WEARING INTIMACY SHOES
IS ALL QUIET
COMPOUNDING

ENANTIO DRAMATIC
SOLUTION BLOWS
TANTRIC FART

SHE BECAME THE ANGEL OF
THE TOWN'S MUSHROOMED
SYMPATHY

OUR BAND CAN IN FACT PLAY YOUR
HYPNOGOGIC
TRANCE RHYTHMS

UP ALL NIGHT WE'RE MAINLY DEAD
OTHER THAN THAT
FEELING FINE

SOURCING IT TENDS TO TRICK US
BELIEVING THAT
WE ARE IT

YEAH CELLARINDA SHE'S GOT
ABANDONMENT
ISSUES DEEP

IS IT TOO LATE TO SAY THAT
WE CAN LEAVE IT
IN GOOD TIME

THEY EXPECT TO BE RELEASED
REAL SOON SPEAKING
COMICALLY

THAT HEART ATTACK YOU KNOW HIS
CONSPIRACY
THEORISM ?

THINK HE'S COOKING IT ALL UP
THAT'S NO LAUGHING
CHICKEN STOCK

SHE'S LOST IT BUT CAN PRACTICE
FOR THE SAKE OF
THE RITUAL

THIS CHURCH SERVICE ATTENDS TO
HYMNODY SLEEP
FELLOWSHIP

3/03/11

THEY THINK THERE IS JUST ONE WAY
OF SEEING IT
THAT 'S JUST FINE

FEELINGS IS WHAT CREATES SONGS
IN MOST CASES
ABOUT BEER

GOVINDA IS PRESENT IN
EVERY YOGA
STUDIO

WILL'S GOT HIS GRAVE STONE PICKED OUT
NOW WANTS THE DATES
TO BE RIGHT

SHALL WE HAVE A PEACH RIGHT NOW
ALL THE GRAPEFRUIT'S
BEEN EATEN ?

IT'S WHAT WE'RE ALL ABOUT HERE
TRANCING AROUND
THIS OLD TOWN

THE BIRD TRIBE WAS HERE EARLY
AND NOW IT'S OUR
SAINT EPHREM

HIS MIND WAS BENT OUT OF SHAPE
FOLLOWING HER
HEART'S YEARNING

3/04/11

IT'S BEEN PROVEN THAT ENHANCED
GETS THE BETTER
OF STYLISH

WE CAN STAY WARMER LONGER
DOING BETTER
WITH NO CHILL

ONCE THIS IS PUBLISHED WE'LL HAVE
FURTHER OPTS FOR
A ROASTING

IS IT NOT WHAT WE HAD THOUGHT
THAT YOU OWNED ALL
THOSE FEELINGS ?

DID WHAT YOU COULD AND NOT WHAT
THEY THOUGHT YOU MEANT
TO HAVE DONE ?

SHE HEARD IN THE DISTANT FOG
IT'S TOO LATE BABE
I'VE MOVED ON

WE CAN LOVE EVERYONE WHEN
THEY HAVE BECOME
CLOSE ENOUGH

THE FLITTERING LITTLE BIRD
NOTIFIES THEM
WHEN TO LEAVE

3/05/11

CROSSING THRESHOLDS BEYOND TIME
WATCHING ALL THINGS
DANCE IN SYNC

IN THE EVENT OF OUR LIVES
COSMIC STREAMS FLOW
THROUGH THIS SPACE

EVERYBODY LOVES WITH WHAT
EVER THEY'VE GOT
TO PROJECT

3/06/11

A NOXIOUS CLOUD EMANATES
FROM THE MASK OF
DECEPTION

SOMETHING ABOUT THIS LOVE SONG
SERVED TO POP THEIR
BRASS BUTTONS

WHICH EAR MIGHT THEY NOW PREFER
FROM THE VAN GOGH
OF POETS ?

YOU KNOW IT MIGHT DAWN ON US
WE'RE LIKE THEM BUT
MUCH CLOSER

WARRIORS APPEAR AS WOLVES
AND THE FLOCK AS
WILD TURKEYS

SO GUILT MAKES US FEEL LIKE WHAT
DO WE OWE WITH
HELL TO PAY ?

WE'VE FAILED AMBIGUITY
PROVIDING THEY'RE
ACCURATE

YOUR HOLINESS CAN FIGURE
WHAT SALVATION
TRULY IS

BRIGHT BLUE INDIGO BUNTING
KEEPS OUR MIND ON
THE RIGHT BIRD

WOLVES ARE STALKING WILD TURKEYS
BIRDS BUSY WITH
THEIR PECKING

THEY'LL TELL YOU ANYTHING JUST
TO EMBRACE YOUR
JOYOUS FACE

VISIONARIES CAN FEEL BLESSED
REVEALING THOUGHTS
IN THE LIGHT

TENDERIZE THE TOUGHNESS WHEN
ATTEMPTING TO
BOND POWER

FEEL BLESSED HAVING ESCAPED FROM
JEALOUS GODS AND
HUNGRY GHOSTS ?

3/08/11

LET US HAVE SOME RESPECT THIS
CAME RIGHT FROM HERE
WHERE IT HURTS

NOTHING'S WRONG WITH RASPUTIN
BUT HE WAS NOT
A SUCCESS

YOU KNOW WHAT WE'RE UP AGAINST
WORK HARD AND STAY
THE COURSE HERE

IT'S PALUNGA TOKO YAH
PHILIPINOS
WE LOVE YOU

3/09/11

WOKE UP FEELING A LITTLE
PEAKED A CHANT
CURES ALL THAT

THIS HERE PURGATORY TEA
ACCOMPLISHES
PURGATION

SO THAT'S OUR CONTRADICTION
WAITING FOR IT
TO HAPPEN ?

THIS IS A WORD PLAY AND NOT
YOUR SIMPLETON'S
PLAY ON WORDS

REALLY UNBELIEVABLE
PEOPLE REFUSE
WHAT THEY ARE

WILL THEY HAVE TO DWELL IN HELL
BECAUSE THEY ARE
THE CHOSEN ?

CAN'T YOU SEE WE'RE EXCITED
AFTER ALL WE'RE
GOING THRU

SOMEONE HERE HAS ASKED ABOUT
YOUR INVOLVEMENT
POTENTIAL

3/10/11

BIKERS FOR JESUS WHAT DO
THEY HAVE IN THEIR
SADDLE BAGS ?

FROM THE FAITH OF RELIGIOUS
REFORM THERE HUNG
ALL THE SAINTS

CHARLES DARWIN'S BIRTHDAY THIS
YEAR'S NATURALLY
SELECTED

WHAT DOES IT TAKE TO FIND THAT
SPECIAL PLACE IN
LONELY HEARTS ?

WE HAVE NO QUALMS ABOUT THE
QUIRKINESS OF
THAT THERE QUARK

THE ESSENCE OF RELIGION'S
GREAT EPITOME
IS ITS TOME

THAT CONDESCENSION AS SUCH
DOES UNDERSCORE
EFFACEMENT

3/12/11

NANO THIS AND NANO THAT
BACTERIA
VIA MARS

THE MUSE KNOWS ENOUGH TO LEAVE
WHEN NOTHING'S LEFT
TO BE DONE

ARRANGEMENTS IN STONE ARE MOST
CERTAINLY NOT
AUTHORED HERE

SHARING SUFFICIENT LOVE TENDS
TO SEND ME TO
BRING FLOWERS

A SAINT KNOWS CONDITIONS OF
PAIN AS WELL AS
FORTITUDE

WHAT WE ARE UP TO AND UP
AGAINST CAN MEAN
A GREAT DEAL

3/13/11

SCIENTISTS ASK HOW MUCH IS
THE UNIVERSE
WORTH TO YOU ?

LOSING HIS HOME HE THOUGHT HOW
ALIEN HE
HAD BECOME

3/14/11

GOD'S LOVE IS OUR FORGIVENESS
HOW OVERTLY
PREDESTINED

WHERE SPIRITUALITY
IS RELIGION
CAN POP UP

THEIR TRANSFERENCE OF GUILT WAS
SO CLEVERLY
ABOLISHED

FAILED TO BE ACCOUNTABLE
NOR COMPLETELY
IN THE KNOW

3/15/11

NOT A CHURCH MINISTER BUT
POLITICAL
REFUGEE

HIS PARENTS TAUGHT HIM ALL HE
KNOWS BUT LOST HIS
RIGHTS TO MUSE

HER LIFE WAS IN DANGER THUS
THE LAW HELD HER
IN HIDING

IS THERE NOTHING OTHER THAN
THIS MYOPIC
CONTRA VERSE ?

ALL THAT GLITTERS IS NOT GOLD
BUT WE CAN NOW
EXTRACT IT

GOVERNMENTS DO ANYTHING
AS LONG AS IT'S
MONITURD

ABSOLUTELY NOTHING LIKE
CONTROVERSY
CAN STOP YOU

YOU KNOW WHEN WE'RE WARRIORS
AND IT'S TO BE
FOR GOD'S SAKE

3/16/11

NEEDS BECOME TOO FILTHY WHEN
CLEANING IS NOT
DONE WITH LIGHT

YOU CAN'T IMAGINE THE CALL
FOR AMBITIOUS
FLUFF MEISTERS

3/17/11

BY VIRTUE OF SILENCE DOES
ETERNAL LOVE
MAGNIFY

FIRST STEP IN RESOLVING ANGST
REALIZATING THE
NEED FOR CHANGE

WE ARE THE DOCTORS OF OUR
OWN DISEASES
DISPELLING

ADVERSITIES ARE REMOVED
CONDITIONED WITH
HARMONY

FOOLISHNESS IS SET UP BY
FALLING INTO
TOO MUCH TALK

MIGHT AS WELL AIM TO BE CALLED
THE FOOL AS TO
STRIVE TO JUDGE

BUDDHISTS KEEP RETURNING SO
ARE THEY IN NEED
OF BUDDHA ?

CAN FEARFULNESS EVER GUIDE
US TO BECOME
WARRIORS ?

REGRESSION IS A PATHWAY
TAKEN FOR SOME
REVISION

3/18/11

IT IS BEST TO SAVE ONE'S SELF
BY LEARNING WHAT
HELPS OTHERS

LOSS WAS THE ONLY WAY THEY
COULD LEARN TO BE
SUCCESSFUL

THE ANDROBOT SAT UPON
HIS GREEN TRACTOR
AND SPED PAST

HALLELUJAH PROCESSION
PROCEEDS TO THE
SOUP KITCHEN

THIS DISH HAS EVERY FLAVOR
THE CHEF MIGHT WANT
TO DREAM UP

3/19/11

PICKING BERRIES CAN LIFT YOU
OUT OF DOLDRUMS
WATCH FOR BUGS

THINK DEFENSIVE THOUGHTS AND THEN
GO AHEAD AND
DISMISS THEM

WE WERE INSIDE ONE OF THOSE
FOR NINE MONTHS MAKES
PERFECT SENSE

THAT HAIR BRAINED STUNT SHE ACCUSED
HIM OF SOMEHOW
JUST BACKFIRED

3/20/11

LOVE SLAYED THE DRAGON THAT FAILED
TO MAKE A FEAST
OF THEIR MINDS

WHO WOULD GO TO FIGHT THAT WAR
ASSUMMING IT'S
FOR NOTHING ?

RUNNING ON EMPTY ARE YOU
CONSIDERING
EMPTINESS ?

ACCOMPLISHING EGOHOOD
IF NOT TELL US
ABOUT IT

IS THERE ANYWAY WE MIGHT
RATIONALIZE TO
MEDIATE ?

3/21/11

EVERY SHAMAN'S SPIRITUAL
RITUAL WANTS TO
RENT THAT BEAR

TWO OPPOSING ENTITIES
DILEMMA OF
POSSESSION

ICON OF A SAINT ACHIEVES
ESTABLISHMENT'S
COMPLETE AWE

ARE THEY CAPABLE OF MORE
VANITY THAN
WE'VE DEALT WITH ?

MADAM I AM ADAM HAVE
YOU MY TICKET
OUT OF HERE?

TOO DEEPLY INGRAINED IN OUR
IGNORANCE TO
SAND IT OUT

IN FORGIVENESS AND RELEASE
DEFENSELESNESS
IS THE RAGE

TRUTH LIES SOME WHERE BETWEEN WHAT
YOU WANT TO HEAR
WHAT THEY SAID ?

THE MIDDLE PATH IS BURIED
DEEP INSIDE YOUR
MIDDLE EARTH

THE SO CALLED NEW AGE HIRED STONED
OPERATION
TECHNOFUNK

SHE'S ON A SPIRITUAL ROLL
DIDACTIC AS
HER ROLE IS

WHAT WERE WE DOING WHEN YOU
GOT LOST TRYING
TO FIND US ?

TRYING TO MAKE SOME SENSE OUT OF
QUESTIONABLE
AGREEMENTS ?

WATCH YOUR FUNNY MONEY THINK
ABOUT SWEARING
OFF MOONSHINE

ASCENDED BEINGS INVITE
COGITATION
WITH HUMANS

3/23/11

JUST A BOWL OF LOBSTER BISQUE
IT'S THE WINNING
BOWL OF SOUP

THE PURPOSE OF BUDDHISM
IS TO MAKE THE
BUDDHA LAUGH

THAT MANY DON QUIXOTES
TO KNOCK DOWN ONE
OLD WINDMILL ?

DHARMA FREE OF AGGRESSION
INSTRUCTS BEYOND
PASSIONATE

WE THINK THE MARTIANS MIGHT WANT
TO CALL THEIR TOWN
GAY PARIS

PERHAPS THERE'S SOMEONE WHO LOVES
US WHOM WE DON'T
KNOW TO LOVE

WE ARE WHOLE AND INNOCENT
ABSOLVED NOW TO
BE RELEASED

WE CAN LOOK WITHIN TO FIND
CREATION'S SWEET
RADIANCE

COME ON NANOBOT PERFORM
FOR US HERE BE
OUR NANNY

THEY CAN'T MAINTAIN THAT STATE WITH
INTROSPECTION
SO TAXING

CAN YOU SEE YOURSELF IN THEIR
SHOES SHOWING THEM
HOW TO WALK ?

3/24/11

MATERIAL SPIRITUAL
TENDANCIES GET
SLICED AND DICED

RACING TOWARDS THE CLIFF EDGE CAN
BE CATCHING TOO
MUCH AFFAIRS

YOU WANT TO BE IN THE LIGHT
YOUR PROBLEM IS
THE LIME LIGHT ?

PROCEDURE FOR CHANGE WILL BE
TO UNROLL THE
SITTING MAT

REMOVAL OF EXTREMES GRANTS
SIGNIFICANT
INVOLVEMENT

PERCEIVES BASIC IRONY
JUXTAPOSED WITH
BORDERLINES

AVOID THOSE TRAPS THAT AIM TO
EVALUATE
HOPES AND FEARS

CREATES SIGNIFICANCE FLOW
BUT CONSIDERS
INERTIA

THE FACT THAT HE DOES SOMETHING
IS A KIND OF
MIRACLE

YOU'VE GOT TO DIG UP THE LOW
ROAD TO SET DOWN
THE HIGHWAY

MOMENTOUS TRANSPARENCY
CORROBORATES
DETACHMENT

YOUR EXTRA TERRESTRIALS
MIGHT PROTECT YOU
FROM THIS THREAT

HE'S NOT A RAPPIST BUT A
MUSICIAN AND
SONGWRITER

MIGHT THEY BE INTERESTED
IN THEIR DHARMA
MUSED THE SAGE ?

THEIR COMPASSIONATE HEALING
RECOGNIZES
REAL PROBLEMS

QUAKED ITS WAY RIGHT INTO OUR
SUPERCONSCIOUS
COLLECTIVE

3/26/11

DID THAT MONSTER DEVELOP
BEYOND IT'S SELF
ENTITY ?

INTERESTED TO FIND OUT
WHAT LIES IN THE
DEPTHS OF MOLD

SHE WAS JUST SOMEBODY WHOM
HE COULD LOVE AND
NOTHING ELSE

IS THERE A TOOL THAT CAN BE
MADE TO WORK THROUGH
SCRAMBLED MINDS ?

REVEAL THAT TRANSITION FROM
BEGINNING TO
PROVOCATE

WHAT IS YOUR CONDITION LIKE
CAN YOU TAKE SOME
ECSTATIC ?

IS THIS SOME CRAZE TO SHIMMY
US AROUND QUITE
LITERALLY ?

THE SIGNIFICANT REPORT
ON THEIR BIG TOE'S
PUZZLEMENT

THAT LOVE WAS NOT COMPASSION
BUT THE CAUSE OF
YOUR PROBLEMS

WE ARE PRONE TO REVEAL OUR
SUBTLE SELF AT
EVERY STAGE

PROVE THAT YOUR MEMORY CAN
RETAIN WORTHWHILE
ENTIRETY

DRESSING UP WITH OUR MUSE IS
THE MOMENT OF
FINERY

WHILE THOSE TWO LITTLE DUFFERS
ARGUE THEY CAN
CONSPIRE TOO

HUMANS DEFINING MARTIAN
D N A ARE
HERE FROM MARS

LIFE'S FILM INVITES EVERYONE
TO EDIT THEIR
OWN SUBSCRIPT

TIME HEALS ALL OUR WOUNDS WHEN YOUR
FORGIVENESS IS
PURPOSEFUL

GIVE THEM SOMETHING FROM THE HEART
SO THEY WON'T MESS
WITH YOUR SOUL

CONTRADICTORY NATURE
INNOVATES QUICK
DEPARTURE

DIVORCED FROM THEIR DELUSIONS
NO LONGER THE
SAME DREAMER

IT MUST BE A STIGMA FROM
THAT LOST EMPIRE'S
BLEEDING HEART

AT LEAST THEY MANAGE TO LOVE
AND GET THEMSELVES
WELL NOTICED

FEELING SO POWERFUL IN
YOGA SENSE STANDS
ON HIS HEAD

POSE A SILLY QUESTION WHEN
THERE ARE NO REAL
SANE ANSWER

BUDDHA AND JESUS ARE A
LOT ALIKE BOTH
FOUND IN HERE

SCIENCE CONFIRMS THIS PLANET
IS NOT REALLY
ALL THIS MULCH

YOU THINK HE LOOKS MORE LIKE A
BOILED EGG AND THAT
SORT OF THING ?

DID HE FALL FOR HER FRUIT CAKE
OR ANGELIC
ABUNDANCE

WHATEVER THEY ARE DOING
SEEMS TO BE DONE
TO THEMSELVES

THIS HEALTH PLAN PREAPPROVES OUR
ANNUAL QUIRK
ADJUSTMENTS

3/28/11

LETTUCE GOES IN THE SALAD
THE FLIES GET WASHED
DOWN THE DRAIN

HAPPY TO SAY THAT THEY WERE
MORE PROUD THAN WE
CAN BELIEVE

MAKE NO MISTAKE ABOUT IT
THAT THERE WAS ONE
BAD BLUNDER

WHY DON'T WE TRY TO MAINTAIN
THE NATURE OF
THOSE CRITTER ?

WE HAVE ONE MINUTE TO WRAP
THIS THING AROUND
YOUR TIRED MIND

IF LAUGHTER'S GOOD ENOUGH THEN
HAVE PLENTY OF
FUN WITH IT

THIS EARTH IS A DIRTY PLACE
BLOW YOUR NOSE AND
WASH YOUR FACE

DO THEY OWN ANY HEAVIES
STOCKHOLM SYNDROME
BABY BLUES ?

3/29/11

THE FRESH AIR WILL DO US GOOD
PLEASE GO OUT THERE
AND FIND SOME

HE ENJOYED YOUR EQUIPMENT
WHAT DID YOU HAVE
TO TELL HIM ?

PLEASE BEAR WITH ME HERE WE WISH
NO OBVIOUS
EXPOSURE

CONSTRUCT NANO CRYSTALS TO
REPLICATE OUR
CHROMOSONES ?

LET'S OFFER THIS COURSE IN THE
COMPARATIVE
SPIRITUAL

IT'S THEIR PROFOUND HABIT TO
KNOCK WHATEVER
THEY FEEL LIKE

3/30/11

RATIONAL THOUGHT OFTEN NEEDS
TO RAMBLE FROM
HERE TO THERE

WHEN TRYING TO GET SOMEWHERE
GIVE UP ONE'S SELF
DECEPTION

PEAKS CLAD IN SNOW CLOUDS FOR HATS
GLOWING WITH THE
SUN AND MOON

BONDED WITH DESOLATION
HE GAVE UP ON
MOUNTAIN TOPS

POEMS LIKE WOLVES AND GREAT CATS
POSSESS THEIR OWN
DISTINCT TALES

ENTERING SELF REFLECTION
KEEP AN EYE ON
THE WHETHER

CUTTING THROUGH CHAIN REACTIONS
THE ULTIMATE
ASCETIC

PROTECTING SNAILS BUT JEALOUS
OF PEOPLE WHERE
DO THEY GO ?

NO MATTER WHAT HUMANS DO
ELEMENTALS TAKE
THEM TO TASK

HAVING SO MUCH FUN WITH HIS
JUNK HE'S MAKING
IT FUNKY

3/31/11

THEIR INQUISITIVENESS CAN'T
TAKE THE PLACE OF
YOUR ESTEEM

IT MUST BE MERE HAPPENSTANCE
WE FIND OURSELVES
LEARNING THIS

THE MOMENT WIND HORSE ARRIVES
WE CAN BECOME
LUMINOUS

WHEN ASKED WHAT HE WANTS SHE SAYS
HE EXPECTS JUST
TO SURVIVE

WHAT HELPED THEM TO FORGET THEIR
MISERY WAS
LAMPOONING

RECLAIMED STATES OF EQUIPOISE
BRINGS OUR PSYCHE
INTO VIEW

HILARIOUSLY AWESOME
BUT ENTIRELY
SCURRILOUS

CHANTING DIVINE PRAISE WITH HE
BHAKTI WALLAH
KIRTAN BLUES

4/01/11

THEY MIGHT NEVER REOPEN
SINCE THE WORLD HAS
BEEN SHUT DOWN

SOME PROVE TOO ELUSIVE WHILE
OTHERS MAKE YOU
STOP TO THINK

4/02/11

YOUR RESERVATIONS HAVE BEEN
CONFIRMED BEYOND
THE BEYOND

THE PROFOUND SMOLDERING LIGHT
IS WHERE HE LIVES
BLISSFULLY

WE'VE TRIED TIME AND TIME AGAIN
IDENTITIES
DON'T EXIST

IN RHETORICAL JEST THE
FAUX NUANCE WAS
REJECTED

ALL THE GHOSTS IN THE WHITE HOUSE
HAVE RECEIVED THEIR
SHADES OF GREY

MILITARY SOLUTIONS
EVENTUALLY
JUST BACKFIRE

EGO LOVES IT WHEN BODY
FEELS GOOD AND FRIENDS
TREAT US FINE

SPIRITUALITY CAN BRING
IN AWFULLY
HIGH END STUFF

4/03/11

NEVER BOTHERED TO ASK ONE
QUESTION OH DEAR
LORD WHY ME ?

MATURE PEOPLE DON'T CONCERN
THEMSELVES WITH THEMES
WHY FAKE IT ?

IT'S THIS PLACE WE'RE PASSING THROUGH
ON OUR WAY TO
KOKOMO

HELD IN THE LIGHT OF EVERY
SENTIENT BEING
SINGS FREEDOM

4/04/11

WHEN WE LEARN WHAT WE HAVE KNOWN
THEN WE KNOW WHAT
WE HAVE LEARNED

4/05/11

THERE IS MORE OLD STYMIED LOVE
OUT THERE THAN YOU'LL
EVER WANT

ELMO CITRO LAH TAH TAH
TAH DEE LAH TAH
TAH DEE TAH

TRIED TO PAY FOR THE SINS OF
THIS WORLD TIME TO
PARTY NOW

THEY'RE AS NUTTY AS A BUNCH
OF FRUIT CAKES GREAT
FLAVORS TOO

THEY CERTAINLY DON'T HAVE MUCH
PREFERENCE UP
THIS OLD CREEK

CONTEMPORARY BELIEF
BOASTS SEVERAL
MIRACLES

TITANS CONCERNED WITH BANNING
HUMANS FROM THEIR
MOTHER EARTH

NO QUESTIONS ASKED ABOUT LOVE
LITTLE OBSERVED
ABOUT LIFE

THEY'RE DOOMED VICARIOUSLY
VIEWING ANCIENT
MIRAGES

THE GREATNESS OF OUR SOUL IS
CONNECTING US
TO HEAVEN

LAUGHING SPONTANEOUSLY
YOU HAVE LEARNED TO
FIND LAUGHTER

IN A SPIRITUAL TREATISE
THERE IS NOTHING
TO COMPARE

WHERE THE MIND CONTAINS EDGES
THERE IS SOMETHING
FARCICAL

HANG ONTO ALL THOSE COLD WARM
DAYS TO KEEP THE
SAP RUNNING

YOU CAN'T IMAGINE WHAT TRUTH
SUPERSEDES NO
REAL PURPOSE

IT'S THE LOVE THAT WE'RE GOING
FOR TO BECOME
ACKNOWLEDGED

HIS ATTEMPT NAILED DOWN ASPIRED
IRONY WITH
FEW RESPECTS

CAN YOU ELUCIDATE THE
FUN SIDE OF YOUR
REFERENCE?

THIS RAMBLING CAN NOT OFFER
A BORING SORT
OF MOMENT

THAT WAS SIMPLY THE MINKY
DEPLOYING ITS
MONKEY MIND

WHY DON'T THEY STRAIGHTEN IT UP
OR AT LEAST TIP
IT OVER ?

ENOUGH CONTROVERSY TO
TO SINK A FLEET OF
DESTROYERS

CAN YOU THINK OF ANYONE
WHO COMPREHENDS
MUDDERS LOVE ?

DUTIFUL SON WAS NOWHERE
WHEN FATHER DIED
TO BE FOUND

THEIR GURU LIKES TO HAVE HIS
IDENTITY
OUTRAGEOUS

PHYLO'S LAW CAN SOLVE PROBLEMS
THAT CREATE MUCH
BIGGER ONES

MOST BEAUTIFUL DIVA DAS
CRAZY WISDOM'S
EVER SEEN

FOUND DOWN IN THE WELL WITH BOTH
HANDS TIED IN A
STATE OF ZEN

IT MUST BE A TERRIBLE
STRAIN ASSUMING
THEY'RE PERFECT

RELEASE ALL OF YOUR SECRETS
AND SEE HOW FAR
THEY CAN FLY

4/06/11

SHE WAS TRYING TO SLAY YOU
NOW AND AGAIN
IS IT GOOD ?

READY FOR BARBECUED STYLE
KARMA SHOVEL
THE TAKE OUT

WHAT WE'RE FEELING IS MERELY
WHAT THEY'RE DOING
SOME WHERE ELSE

4/07/11

NOW THAT'S THE BOTTOM LINE AND
THE FIDDLER PLAYS
ANOTHER

SORRY IDOL DIDN'T MEAN
TO USE A BRUSH
WITH PAINT DRIPS

THE RAP CONCERT'S WINDING DOWN
WHO CAN ABSORB
MORE HATE LOVE ?

TITANS ARE INVADING AND
OUR BIRD TRIBE'S FIT
TO BE TIED

4/08/11

BEGINNINGS DO MULTIPLY
PROFUSIONS OF
PROGENY

LOVE IS A PURE SOURCE OF JOY
CONFUSE IT NOT
WITH PASSION

4/09/11

KRISHNA LETS THEM KNOW WHEN TO
START THE CHANT WITH
OM NAMO

REMEMBER YOUR ORTZEL PHRASE
YOU MIGHT WANT TO
COIN IT NOW

HE HAS FAITH IN EVERYTHING
HEALING HIMSELF
WITH THE MUSE

INTRIGUES DO NOT CONSTITUTE
DEVOTION TO
DIVINE ONES

CAN INTUITION TELL US
WHEN JESUS IS
RETURNING ?

LIFE IS SIMPLE ENOUGH THOUGH
CULTURE DOES NOT
EXIST THERE

THE DEEPER WE GO THE MORE
BEAUTY WE FIND
SO DIG IN

PURE ENERGY ARISES
TO PROCESS FULL
ALIGNMENT

TRANSMUTATION RELOCATES
ENJOYABLE
AWARENESS

THOUGHT UNENCUMBERED BY YOUR
REASON IGNITES
THE CHAKRAS

HAPPIEST WHEN OUR HIGHEST
SELF TELLS US WHERE
WE'RE GOING

APOLOGIZE FOR EATING
THAT PIE BUT DON'T
FEEL REMORSE

WE ARE PASSING THROUGH MY SPACE
IN SEARCH OF THE
SOURCE OF LOVE

RINPOCHE'S LESSON INCLUDES
A MUSING MIND
TRANSMISSION

APART FROM THESE OBSESSIONS
THEY'RE COMPLETELY
DELIGHTFUL

SEEMS LIMERICKS HAVE TAKEN
LITTLE HOLIES
UNAWARES

THE ONE WHO CHANGES DARKNESS
INTO LIGHT KNOWS
HOW TO GROOVE

WE FOUND YOUR HUNGRY BEAR WAS
EATING APPLES
AROUND HERE

HERE BOY GOOD BOY COME HERE YOU
LITTLE DOGGY
PRO BONO

4/10/11

CESSATION OF DESIRE DOES
NOT MEAN THERE'S NO
FUTURE HERE

4/11/11

FORGIVENESS OF THE SELF CURES
SEPARATION'S
DELUSIONS

WINE MADE FROM FERMENTATION
OF OUR DIVINE
POTENTIAL

A SPECK IN THE EYE CAN GROW
QUITE A LARGE LOG
OVER TIME

HERE COME BABA AND BABET
DOTING ON OUR
BABINI

IN PEARLS OF UNDERSTANDING
IRRITATION
BECOMES LOVE

ACKNOWLEDGING IGNORANCE
CONTRARY TO
OUR BELIEFS ?

FILES LABELLED CONFIDENTIAL
FOR CONFIDENT
CONFIDANTS

MANY HAVE PRETENDED TO
BE RECLUSIVE
FEW PURELY

CONTEMPLATION IN STILLNESS
BRINGS REASONABLE
CONTENTMENT

NO ONE CAN EVER SELL OUT
AND HAVE WHAT THEY
TRULY WANT

US DIEHARDS CAN PERCEIVE AS
FAR AS OUR OWN
MIND CONTROLS

WOLVES IN RED RIDING HOODS WORLD'S
GONE TO HELL IN
HAND BASKET'S

IF LOVE AND TRUTH FOLLOWS US
WE ARE TRULY
GLORIFIED

WAS IT REALLY A MARRIAGE
THAT ENVIOUS
INTERLUDE ?

FELL INTO THE RIVER EACH
TIME THEY TRIED YOUR
POINT OF VIEW

THIS LESSON IN CONFUSION
THAT'SALL TODAY
BOYS AND GIRLS

YAH YAH GANOW IS ALL THE
FARMER HAD TO
SAY ON THAT

THE FEAR OF DEATH CANNOT CAUSE
EVERY DESIRE
ON THIS EARTH

4/12/11

THAT DUMB SHOW OF ELEPHANTS
IS HOW BO GOT
APPOINTED

DESTINY HAS NO PLAN FOR
YOUR INSURANCE
STRATEGY

THE PIE EATING CONTEST WAS
A WAKE UP CALL
MUCH LATER

AN INDEPENDENT SOURCE CLAIMS
IT IS TO BE
CONTINUED

THAT WAS A GREAT PIECE OF QUICHE
MUCH CONDOLENCE
FOR THE CAKE

THIS HAS THE PLAINTIVE NOTE OF
MASS MIGRATIONS
DEPARTING

DON'T YOU WORRY ABOUT A
DOG GONE THING THAT'S
A GOOD PUP

THEY SIT BACK ON THEIR LAURELS
WHILE HE MAKES OFF
WITH THE CROWN

YOU MIGHT CALL IT SEPARATE
REALITY
CONSCIOUSNESS

THEY WERE GONERS HE ALONE
SURVIVED ABJECT
CERTAINTY

WHAT IS THIS ENTITY THAT
OFFERS THEM MIND
TRANSMISSION ?

GO ON NOW GET OUT THERE AND
FILL THE COSMOS
STARS' BURNING

4/13/11

YO CO EMERGENT WISDOM
REVOLVING DOORS
OF KARMA

A LITTLE HOT BENEATH THE
COLLAR GET A
HOSE ON IT

NOT GOING THERE IS THE BEST
PLACE FOR US TO
BE RIGHT NOW

HAVENS OF DISCURSIVE THOUGHT
ABANDONED WHEN
TIME STANDS STILL

ARE TURKEYS ARE BECOMING
WOLVES THAT HUNT FOR
MORE TURKEYS ?

4/14/11

PEACEFUL WARRIORS SUCCEED
DISENTANGLING
ENGAGED ONES

THEY BECOME HIS FRIENDS WHEN HE
APPEARS TO BE
FILLED WITH EASE

HIS BROTHER IS A HEAVY
HE HIMSELF IS
NOT TOO FAT

COURAGE CANNOT SIMPLY BE
A VIRTUE IT
DEVOURS ALL

4/15/11

OUR SIXTH SENSE TENDS TO LURE US
INTO TRAPS AND
SOLVES PROBLEMS

PEACEFUL WARRIORS SUCCEED
WHERE ANGRY ONES
LEAVE CONFUSED

NO ONE LIKES HIM DUE TO HIS
POSITION IN
SHOCK AND AWE

THERE CAN BE NO SUFFERING
WHERE SHAKTIPAT'S
TAKEN HOLD

SHE WASN'T LAUGHING AT YOU
TICKLED ONLY
BY HER MUSE

TAKE A HIKE TODAY SO YOUR
NATURAL CADENCE
IS MAINTAINED

4/16/11

GIVE UP ILLUSIONS OR LOSE
THE HARMONIC
CONVERGENCE

HIKING ON SEPARATE PATHS
THEIR SEARCH COMPLETES
THE CIRCLE

PUT ASIDE OUR SCRUTINY
THIS MOMENTOUS
OCCASION

EXPERIENCE YOUR PRESENT
ATTITUDE WITH
NO PROBLEM

4/17/11

IF YOU MAKE IT IN SAINT JAY
YOU HAVE MADE IT
ANYWAY

SHE MIGHT HAVE BEEN THE PERFECT
WOMAN FOR HIM
JUST KIDDING

HE ASSUMES THAT SHE'S IN LOVE
BUT THAT IS HIS
BIG MISTAKE

HE HAS NOT FALLEN FOR HER
FANTASIES SHE'S
HIDDEN THEM

NO ONE SEEMS TO SWEAT IT WHEN
THEY HAVE BECOME
ENLIGHTENED

THEIR EXCEPTIONAL MARRIAGE
TURNED OUT TO BE
A THRILLER

4/18/11

WE WILL FIND LOVE DEEP WITHIN
BEHOLD IT NOW
AND AGAIN

TO BE ADMIRED BY THEM YOU
MUST HAVE YOUR PETS
AND FAMILY

IT IS COMIC TO BE IN
THIS INNOCENCE
TOGETHER

LOVE IS WHAT DISPELS THE FEAR
OF HAVING NOT
ENOUGH LOVE

MUST YOU PROJECT MORE PITY
PROVING TO THEM
THEY'RE SORRY ?

4/22/11

IT'S NO BIG DEAL SEEMS TO BE
IN TRUTH NOTHING
EVER WAS

MAKING SOME SENSE OF CRAZY
WISDOM BELIES
SEDUCTION

HATCHING INGENIOUS PLOTS THEIR
FANTASTIES PROVED
SUBSTANTIAL

4/24/11

IT'S NOT THAT WE CAN'T CHANGE OUR
MINDS BUT HOW YOUR
MIND CAN CHANGE

IF THERE WERE JUST A BODY
HE COULD TELL HIS
TROUBLES TO

SUN'S BEEN SETTING OVER THERE
FOR A NUMBER
OF YEARS NOW

4/25/11

INDICATIVE INSTRUCTIONS
TO BOTTLE IT
MERRILY

MY GUESS IS THAT WE ALL ARE
ADDICTS AND THAT'S
WHY WE'RE HERE

THEIR RECIPE FOR PEACE BAKES
BOOMERS' BOISTEROUS
PROGENY

4/26/11

GOOD BIRDS LOSE FEATHERES WHEN A
PETTY TYRANT
RULES THE ROOST

WHAT EVER YOU DO DON'T YOU
TRY AND GRAB IT
BY THE TAIL

STILLNESS SIGNS ETERNITY'S
SIGNATURE IN
SOLITUDE

SILENCE FINDS A WEALTH OF GOLD
FUNDING TO USE
AS PAYMENT

CHANTS PROVIDE STIMULATION
WITH POSITIVE
ABSORPTION

THEIR TIME TOGETHER WAS SPENT
LIKE BATS HANGING
IN THE CAVE

DOES IT MATTER WHAT THEY ARE
THINKING ABOUT
YOUR ACTIONS ?

THERE IS THE APPRAISER WHO
EVALUATES
NON JUDGEMENT

4/27/11

INVOKING BASIC GOODNESS
INSPIRES ANGER
INTO LOVE

YOUR SONGS OF AWAKENING
HAVE BEEN RAISED UP
THIS MORNING

MANKIND HAS TO GROW UP AND
STOP MAKING SUCH
A BIG MESS

WHEN ATTEMPTING TO CARVE A
PARADIGM WILL
YOU CUT IT ?

IT'S NOT REALLY CARVED IN STONE
JUST HAPPENS TO
LOOK LIKE THAT

4/28/11

THE MOST MUNDANE SACRED TEXT
HAS IMMERSION
MAGNETIZED

THUS THE SPRINGTIME SETTING WITH
SUNRISE AND PEACH
TREES IN BLOOM

HE MIGHT HAVE BEEN THAT FARM BOY
WORKING HARD TO
RAISE THOSE PIGS

HE FELT HE GOT THE AX WHEN
NO ONE AXED HIM
WHAT HE'D DONE

SOMEONE HAD SUGGESTED WHAT'S
TO BE DONE WITH
NOTHINGNESS

4/29/11

LIFE FORMS YOUR PERCEPTIONS TO
GAUGE LOGICAL
DIMENSIONS

HE CLIMBED TO THE TOP BUT COULD
NOT SEE IT FROM
ITS SUMMIT

CAN THERE BE NO HIGHEST SELF
HIGHER THAN OUR
OTHER SELVES ?

RELIES ON VISITATIONS
TO EXAMINE
FEARLESSNESS

SAINTS NEED NOTHING TO ENTER
THE DOMINION
OF HEAVEN

4/30/11

RECALL TO MIND DEVOTION
CONSIDER THE
RADIANCE

CAN'T SAY ANYTHING ABOUT
THAT MESSAGE OF
SECRECY

SING PRAISES TO ALL SENTIENT
BEINGS BEFORE
YOU ABSCOND

DIVING INTO THE TIMELESS
DEPTHS OF MERMAID'S
DARKLING REALM

5/01/11

LET US HAVE NO SOUL BASHING
PROVIDING WE'RE
INNOCENT

5/02/11

WE DON'T LIKE TO PUSH BUTTONS
THEN AGAIN WHAT
IS IN THERE ?

WHENEVER WE SEE SUNSHINE
SHE IS OUTDOORS
AND FINDS US

YOU LIKE TO EXPERIMENT
BUT WHO IS THE
GUINEA PIG ?

THAT IS NEWS TO EVERYONE
INCLUDING ME
BE IT SO

MAMMY SLAMMY WHAMMY BEE
BLESSED WITH HER HOME
HARMONY

5/03/11

CAN'T ADMIT TO THEIR PROBLEMS
DON'T KNOW THEM WE
HAVEN'T MET

GOOD GRACIOUS HOW ENHANCING
NOT TO MENTION
HEART WRENCHING

NOT EASILY EMBARRASSED
CAN GUIDE US TO
SHAMELESSNESS

THE PROBLEM WITH PRIDE IS THAT
FEAR MUST THEN BE
FORGIVEN

GO FAR BEYOND THE TRAIL LET
NOT YOUR PATH BE
LEFT BEHIND

WE'VE GOT TO TACKLE SOMETHING
THAT WILL DRAG US
ALL THE WAY

SPIGOTS HAVE MUCH TO LEARN BY
POURING FORTH THEIR
IGNORANCE?

5/04/11

WHAT SEEMS INSIGNIFICANT
CARRIES WEIGHT FROM
YOUR SHOULDERS

DREAMS AREN'T MUCH TO PEOPLE WHOSE
GOOD INTENTIONS
ARE COMPLETE

5/08/11

THEY WON'T BE HAPPY UNTIL
SOMEONE FINDS THEIR
PERFECT SELF

HAVING YOUR DESIRE DEVOURED
IS ABOUT TO
TAKE THE CAKE

WE ARE THIS CLOSE AND THAT FAR
FROM ACHIEVING
THE END POINT

MORALIZING TEARS SHREDS CLOTH
FROM THE SUIT OF
PURE KNOWING

NOW WE'VE VAPORIZED THEY WANT
PERMISSION TO
SUBLIMATE

THIS LATEST MIND TRANSMISSION
FEELS LIKE ROLLING
OFF A LOG

5/10/11

HUMANS FIND DILEMMAS TO
TEACH US HOW TO
RELEASE THAT

ANOTHER'S CONCERN FOR US
MELTS THE HEART LIKE
SNOW IN MARCH

5/11/11

THE GLASS THAT IS STAINED MIGHT LOOK
NICE STANDING IN
THE WINDOW

YOUR ELOCUTIONIST CHOSE
TO SUBMIT TO
HOWLING WOLVES?

IT RIPPED HERE'S A HUNDRED BUCKS
LET'S GO FIND SOME
NEW USED RAG

TWAS THE BLEAT OF THE BLACK SHEEP
IN YOUR SLEEP WE
KID YOU NOT

CONTROVERSY SUBDUCTING
MINDS AT THE FRINGE
FESTIVAL

5/12/11

DISCHARGING HILARITY
WHILE STANDING AT
HEAVEN'S GATE

NOW LOOK AT WHAT YOU'VE DONE THAT
DREAM PERCEPTION
HAD NO FLAWS

5/14/11

WE'RE CERTAIN THAT HE'S TAKING
THE RIGHT TURN OR
SOMETHING ELSE

THE FACT IS SHE WAS HEALED WHILE
SINGING THE OM
SHIVA CHANT

ENLIGHTENMENT CAN EXPLAIN
AWAY THE SENSE
OF TRAUMA

LADS RELATE MORE TO THAT WILD
SURREPTITIOUS
BEHAVIOR

WAS IT THE UNIVERSE OR
ITS THEORY LAID
THIS LARGE EGG ?

WORDS DESIGNED TO EDUCATE
NOT TO CONFOUND
NOR CONDEMN

5/18/11

HEY LITTLE BEAR WAKE UP TIME
GET GOING SPRING
HAS NOW SPRUNG

WE DON'T KNOW WE'RE IN LOVE YET
BECOME AWARE
AND WE MAY

5/20/11

HE'S NOT SO THICK SKINNED BUT HAS
RATIONALES FOR
EVERYTHING

BE WATCHFUL AND JAH WILL GRANT
US ALMIGHTY
PROTECTION

GOLLY MOLLY WORDS DON'T MEAN
A THING 'LESS YOUR
HEART'S IN IT

PEERING OUT THE OPENED DOOR
SURPRISING TREES
LEAFED IN GREEN

ANYTHING YOU WANT TO DO
WITH THESE PICKING'S
FINE WITH ME

FINAL WORDS HAVE BEEN RESERVED
FOR NO UNDO
FACULTY

FRIENDS WRITE BOOKS ON POLITICS
CAREFUL NOT TO
BEFOUL THEM

CHERRY PLUM HAVE YOU DISMISSED
THAT CONTROLLING
BEHAVIOR ?

OUR SHARED FREQUENCIES PROVIDE
GUIDANCE FOR THE
JOYOUS ONE

YOU KNOW YOU CAN LOVE YOURSELF
WE'RE NEVER HERE
ALL ALONE

DIVINE LOVE IS OF ITSELF
AND CAN BE SHARED
LIKE IT IS

WHO KNOWS WHERE THE GREAT SAINTS ARE
MUST BE HIDDEN
HERE SOMEWHERE

www.ingramcontent.com/pod-product-compliance
Lightning Source LLC
Chambersburg PA
CBHW051817090426
42736CB00011B/1526